REEL SUCCESS

REEL SUCCESS:
CREATING DEMO REELS AND ANIMATION PORTFOLIOS

CHERYL CABRERA

Routledge
Taylor & Francis Group

LONDON AND NEW YORK

First published 2013
by Focal Press

2 Park Square, Milton Park, Abingdon, Oxon OX14 4RN
711 Third Avenue, New York, NY 10017, USA

Routledge is an imprint of the Taylor & Francis Group, an informa business

First issued in hardback 2017

Library of Congress Cataloging in Publication Data

CIP data has been applied for.

ISBN: 978-0-240-82102-3 (pbk)
ISBN: 978-1-138-42858-4 (hbk)

Typeset in Rotis Sans Serif
Project Managed and Typeset by: diacriTech

www.reelsuccess.com

Bound to Create

You are a creator.

Whatever your form of expression — photography, filmmaking, animation, games, audio, media communication, web design, or theatre — you simply want to create without limitation. Bound by nothing except your own creativity and determination.

Focal Press can help.

For over 75 years Focal has published books that support your creative goals. Our founder, Andor Kraszna-Krausz, established Focal in 1938 so you could have access to leading-edge expert knowledge, techniques, and tools that allow you to create without constraint   We strive to create exceptional, engaging, and practical content that helps you master your passion.

Focal Press and you.

Bound to create.

We'd love to hear how we've helped
you create. Share your experience:
www.focalpress.com/boundtocreate

DEDICATION

This book is dedicated to my students,
past, present, and future,
as well as aspiring artists
and animators around the world.
This book is written for you.

and
in loving memory of my mother,
Jo Ann K. Cookmeyer

CONTENTS

ACKNOWLEDGEMENTS

Special thanks to the following people for their help during this entire process:

A special thanks to Caitlin Murphy, my editorial project manager, and David Bevans, Lauren Mattos, and Katy Spencer, my supportive and phenomenal acquisition editors at Focal Press. Their encouragement and confidence saw me through this entire journey and through every obstacle I encountered. I will be forever thankful for their support!

I want to thank my friends who have contributed their amazing artwork and words of wisdom, most of them former students and classmates of mine. Without them, this book would not have become so dimensional: David Bokser, Chris Brown, Sean Buck, Marcos Carrasco, Ashley DeMattos, Lauryn Duerr, Chris Jaser, Matt Justice, Bridget Kieffer, Heather Knott, Paul Krause, Joey Lenz, Melissa Massingill, Reece Mayer, Michael Milano, Hannah Moon, Aaron Morse, Marcelo Nader, Phillip Negroski, Rey Ortiz, Tonya Payne, Juan Rivera, Joe Rosa, Harrison Stark, Randy Stratton, Matt Sullivan, Becki Tower, Ben Willis, Jamex Xu, and Wei-Shan Yu.

Thanks to Tonya Payne, my technical editor, friend, former student, and inspiration. Her quick and thorough feedback was amazing.

Thanks to Joe Pasquale, my mentor and friend, for teaching me so much about this industry and guiding me when I created my first VHS demo reel and packaged portfolio.

Thanks again to not only the students but also the faculty, staff, and administration of the School of Visual Arts and Design and the College of Arts and Humanities at the University of Central Florida, for their constant support and questions of "How's the book going?" Extra special thanks to my colleagues and mentors: JoAnne Adams, Darlene Hadrika, Phil Peters, MC Santana, Stella Sung, and Natalie Underberg-Goode.

A special thanks to all my family and friends who have supported me through a very tumultuous time of my life, losing my mother to cancer and going through a divorce, which happened to coincide with the writing of this book. An extra special thanks to my brother, Eugene N. Cookmeyer II, sister-in-law Marlene Mueller, step-father George Tripkovich, soon to be daughter-in-law Taylor Roberson, cousin Vickie Dauphin Dewey, and Aunt Kathleen Ballweber. And in no particular order, my dearest friends Darlene Marr, Bob Owens, June and Bill Hackworth, Heather Knott, Virginia Kepner, Nancy and Hal Miles, Lucilla Hoshor, Jeanna and Joey Dysart, Penny Clarke Johnson, Tracie King, Tom Mavor, Randy and Ann Asprodites, Dana Niedergall, Dave Kaul, Lauren Lapointe, Heidi Poche, and Susan Weaver. Their love, support, and endless hours talking on the phone during my commute have proven to be invaluable to me. I don't know what I would have done or what I would do without them.

A heart-filled thanks to Marcos Carrasco, for helping me find my creative passion again and for showing me true love.

A super-duper special thanks to my children, Joshua and Nathanael, who give me a reason to wake up every morning and never give up.

Most importantly, I thank God, for His continued guidance and for giving me the ability to live my life with strength and grace.

PREFACE

I've been teaching animation for 12 years. Every day I talk to students about how to put together a demo reel and portfolio package. I write recommendations, do workshops, teach classes and have never been able to refer students to a book on the subject, because one never existed, until now. I am thankful to my publisher, Focal Press, for the opportunity to create this book.

I can't write this book without talking about the digital elephant in the room. The animation and visual effects industries are going through a tense time right now, and hopefully some sort of metamorphosis is going to happen for the better. This isn't anything new, really. Since I've been involved in this industry for the past 14 years, there has been an ebb and flow fluctuation of hirings and firings, and I've heard many stories from colleagues and friends who have been in this industry much longer than I have. It's time for the Phoenix to burn and rise again from its ashes.

Regardless of the current climate of our industry, we must continue to strive to be better artists and animators and try not to let this situation unnerve new artists and animators from entering the field. We must keep our standards high and set the bar higher. We must remember to never work for free no matter how much we want to work on a particular project. Our art form requires highly trained and talented people. We deserve to be treated as respected employees and not as indentured servants.

I truly hope this book helps you along your journey. I have created a website to support this book for FAQs and other postings. The website contains sample portfolios of actual student demo reels that landed jobs right out of school, as well as some that did not with a critique of what could have been done better.

You can see what has been done before and what actually works! There is also a forum area where you can post your reel for feedback. Please make sure to visit and check things out: www.reelsuccess.com

ABOUT THE AUTHOR

Cheryl Cabrera has advised and guided aspiring animators, game artists, and visual effects artists since 2001. Currently teaching all aspects of production in the Character Animation specialization as an assistant professor of digital media at the University of Central Florida, she also taught as professor of animation at the Savannah College of Art and Design from 2001 to 2009. Cheryl is currently on the Board of Directors for the Animation Hall of Fame. She is a digital artist and animator who blends the lines between digital imagery and the traditional painting medium. She has participated in numerous group and solo exhibitions in the United States, and her works are featured in several private collections. Cheryl is also an Autodesk Certified Instructor in Maya and author of *An Essential Introduction to Maya Character Rigging*. She is a current member of SIGGRAPH, the Society for Animation Studies, and Women in Animation.

INTRODUCTION

Sometimes things become possible if we want them bad enough.

—T.S. Eliot

The reason I am writing this book is to give an honest look at how to get your foot into the door of the animation industry. My intention is to be direct and to the point. What is expected and what is reality.

The first thing that I want to establish is that this book is not the answer to all your questions. The animation industry is constantly in flux and change happens as fast as technology. So while I've done my best to represent what I've learned throughout the past 13 years, I hope you realize that even as you read this there may be some changes happening that aren't implemented in this book. I hope to represent as many different opinions and voices as I could.

I am a strong believer that whatever dreams you really want to achieve in life can be achieved if you persist on your path toward those dreams. Occasionally, you have to put your dreams on hold while you deal with some of the curve balls that life throws at you. Sometimes you should realize that your abilities do not match the current demand or competition. In this situation, you must continue to work at building your skills. That being said let me also say that no one should ever stop you from pursuing your dreams. If you want something, then you have to keep your eye on the goal and continue to work hard toward achieving that goal. I've seen people graduate and walk straight into an animation apprenticeship at PIXAR, and I've seen people graduate and take anywhere from 6 to 10 years before they get their first studio position. I've also seen many who just give up or decide that this industry is really not for them.

Just because you are fresh out of college or new to the industry does not mean you don't have as good of a chance as someone who has been working out in LA for a while. Because, quite frankly, you are probably more enthusiastic, cheaper, and come along with fresh ideas and raw talent; hence, many studios are willing to give you an opportunity to prove yourself. Just remember, looking for a job is a full time job in itself. The need for talent in the animation industry ebbs and flows. Many factors affect the job market so be patient and persistent. Continue to improve your skills and talent.

Please check out the companion website www.reelsuccess.com for color versions of all the images in this book, demo reels, source files, and much, much more.

CHAPTER 1

THE DESIGN OF SELF-PROMOTION

Keep your dreams alive. Understand to achieve anything requires faith
and belief in yourself, vision, hard work, determination, and dedication.
Remember all things are possible for those who believe.

—Gail Devers

THE ART OF SELF-PROMOTION

I want to begin this book and this chapter with the idea that first you must
believe in yourself. If you don't, who will? We can compare the process of
trying to get your foot in the door of any job with that of dating and finding
a spouse, or building any relationship, really. Most of the rules apply to both.
In a way you're trying to sell yourself to a potential romantic partner just as
you are trying to sell yourself to a potential employer. So there are some key
concepts that you must keep in mind and they are as follows:

Show your value. How are you different from everyone else? What
makes you the cream of the crop? Why are you worth the investment
of time? Don't just blabber on about how wonderful and great you are.
Prove it. Everything you do from this point forward in creating the best
representation of yourself should illustrate how creative you are and
show your talents and abilities. Learn how to problem-solve. Problem
solving is probably the most important skill that you can have.

Show the best version of yourself without being phony or fake.
The old adage of put your best foot forward definitely applies here.
Be professional. Take time to groom yourself both physically and
professionally. Have class. Show style. Show that you're a fun person to
be around. Establish that you work well and play well with others. If you
present yourself as something you are not, you may get the job, but you
won't be able to keep it. The animation industry is very connected, and
this information travels quickly.

> It is not the strongest of the species that survives, nor the most intelligent, but the one most responsive to change.
>
> Charles Darwin

Be confident, don't be arrogant. Know your abilities. Know your strengths but also know your weaknesses and be willing to work on those. Be humble. Be polite. Don't minimize yourself and don't put others down. Be open to ideas and suggestions. Don't be defensive when someone critiques you or your work.

Be open to change. Be open to ask questions. Accept the fact that this industry is in flux constantly. Show that you are flexible. Being able to remain calm and not let change upset you is extremely important.

Be focused and on target, but remember to look at the big picture. Know what you want to do. Everything you do should be done with that goal in mind. If you don't know what you want to do, then you will come across as both indecisive and unsure of yourself and your abilities. Realize that where you want to be may be out of reach at this moment, but continue to make decisions that will eventually lead you to where you want to go. Don't get frustrated. Don't give up. Keep on working toward that goal and you will eventually get there.

Don't waste anyone's time. Get to the point. Always be clear, be concise, be passionate, do your best, and stay on target.

Be willing to continue to work on improving both yourself and your portfolio. Don't burn yourself out. Stay motivated. Do things that help you stay inspired. Stay fresh. Get away from the computer. Be joyful. Get involved in your community. Stay active. Find a cause. Find a hobby. Take a class. Play games. Go to the movies for fun not to critique—leave that for the critics. Do something that brings life into who you are and what you do. Let your experience inspire your work and keep it fresh. Stop hanging around with people in your life who pull you down or squash your hopes and dreams. Fill your life with people who inspire you. Find balance and happiness.

DESIGN

There are plenty of books out there that talk about design and self-promotion. At the end of this chapter, I have listed a few that I've used, and I highly recommend them. This chapter defines a few basic rules and things you need to consider when it comes to logo, business card, letterhead, and website design, so that you can do it on your own, especially if you don't have the money to hire a designer.

So, why bother designing your portfolio? First, it shows that you are serious about your profession, and a unified, nicely designed portfolio looks professional. So, where do you start?

Probably the most important thing you have to decide when designing for self-promotion is who you are and how you want to be represented. How will you represent yourself visually? What is your style?

You should begin by asking yourself: What adjectives do you use to describe yourself?

Make a list of words that describe who you are. The following is a word bank of adjectives that you can use to help describe yourself and figure out how you want to represent yourself visually.[1] This is a good start.

A abnormal action active adaptive adolescent agreeable aggressive aesthetic agrarian alert alluring ambiguous ambitious amusing animated annoying antique anxious appealing archival arctic artistic athletic atypical authoritative automated avant-garde awkward **B** basal basic beautiful bizarre black bland boisterous boundless brave brazen brief bright brilliant **C** calm captivating chaotic charm childlike choice classic classical cluttered coherent colorful cool comic compassionate compelling complicated confident conservative contemporary conventional convincing cooperative corporate creative cryptic cultured cutting-edge **D** dark dated dazzling delicate dependable dirty disheveled disordered distinctive drab drive dynamic **E** eager elaborate electric elegant emotional empathetic endurable energy enthusiasm enticing essential evil exciting excited extraordinary extreme **F** factual faint fancy fast feminine fine flamboyant flashy fleeting friendly fresh frigid fundamental fussy **G** gaudy gender-specific generous generational glitzy gloomy goal-oriented graceful gusto **H** happy harmonious heavy hidden high-tech hilarious historical hostile hued humorous **I** illustrative imaginative immediate impressive indecisive infantile innocent innovative instantaneous intelligent intense intricate inventive invigorating **J** jazzy juvenile **K** kinetic knowledgeable **L** lethargic laughable lavish light lively logical loud ludicrous **M** macho magnetic majestic manly masculine maternal maximum mechanical melodious memorable messy meticulous minimal moderate modern morbid muted mysterious **N** naïve native natural needy new nominal nostalgic Nosy **O** obscure observant obsessive old ominous oomph organic ornate ostentatious out-of-the-ordinary **P** placid passionate past pastel persuasive peaceful pizazz plain pleasant polite powerful prime productive psychedelic punch pure **Q** quick quiet quixotic

R rare raw refined religious retro rich refreshing relaxed reminiscent representative responsible resonant retrospective revolutionary righteous robotic romantic **S** serene showy sloppy small soft somber soothing spiritual staid strong stylish suggestive swift symbolic **T** tacky tawdry techno tempting terse traditional typographic **U** ultimate uncommon uncultivated undeveloped unkempt unpolished unusual **V** vague verve and vigor vigorous vintage **W** wacky warm well-known whimsical whispered wild witty womanly **Y** young youthful **Z** zing.

Once you have your list, you now have to narrow down by using your creativity to visualize what these adjectives mean. Here are some suggestions and clever ideas to get your creative juices flowing.

USE YOURSELF

There is no better way to represent yourself and your style than to use something from what you have already created or to create something specifically to represent yourself. This is where your design should begin. Start looking through your own artwork with a different angle. Is there something that you have already created that can be used as in Figure 1.1? You should figure out what is your very best work and pull an image or idea from that. What better way to introduce yourself than with your very best creation? How about objects that represent your personality or identity? Perhaps you always wear a certain hat or glasses. Do you have a nicely drawn caricature of yourself or self-portrait as in Figure 1.2? Perhaps you have created a computer graphics (CG) version of yourself? What about a visual play or word play with your name as in Figure 1.3? Your monogram or initials as in Figure 1.4? How about creating a logo that shows your chosen specialty as in Figure 1.5?

Figure 1.1 *An Example Business Card for an Animator Who Used One of Her Characters as Her Identity for Self-Promotion*

BORROW FROM THE MASTERS

The number 1 rule in being an artist is learn from the masters. Be inspired by real designers or artists. Borrow from them. Find something visual that you

Figure 1.2 An Example Business Card of a Self-Portrait Character of the Animator

Figure 1.3 An Example Business Card With a Nice Visual Play of This Person's Last Name, Which Happens to be Moon

Figure 1.4 An Example Business Card With a Fun Interpretation of This Person's Initials, RPM

Figure 1.5 An Example Business Card of a Rigger

love. Take something that is already working and make it your own. Now I'm not saying to infringe on anyone's copyright, but what I am saying is what artists have done from the very beginning: appropriate and be inspired by something that is already out there. Below is an alphabetical list of art movements, followed by an alphabetical list of materials and techniques. Perhaps an artist during one of these movements fits your style, or maybe a particular material or technique will spark an idea.

List of Art Movements
A – Abstract Art – Art Brut – Abstract expressionism – Abstract illusionism – Academic Art – Action Painting – Aestheticism – Altermodern – American Barbizon School – American Impressionism – American Realism – American Scene Painting – Analytical Art – Antipodeans – Anti-Realism – Arabesque – Arbeitsrat für Kunst – Art Deco – Art Informel – Art Nouveau – Art Photography – Arte Povera – Arts and Crafts Movement – Ashcan School – Assemblage – Les Automatistes – Auto-Destructive Art – **B** – Barbizon School – Baroque – Bauhaus – **C** – Classical Realism – Color Field – Context Art – Computer Art – Concrete Art – Conceptual Art – Constructivism – Cubism – **D** – Dada – **E** – Expressionism – **F** – Fantastic Realism – Fauvism – Figurative Art – Figuration Libre – Folk Art – Fluxus – Futurism – **G** – Geometric Abstract Art – Graffiti – Gutai Group – **H** – Harlem Renaissance – Humanistic Aestheticism – Hypermodernism – Hyperrealism – Impressionism – **I** – Institutional Critique – International Gothic – International Typographic Style – **L** – Les Nabis – Letterism – Lowbrow (art movement) – Lyco Art – Lyrical Abstraction – **M** – Magic Realism – Mannerism – Massurrealism – Maximalism – Metaphysical Painting – Mingei – Minimalism – Modernism – Modular Constructivism – **N** – Naïve Art – Neoclassicism – Neo-Dada – Neo-expressionism – Neo-figurative – Neoism – Neo-primitivism – Net Art – New Objectivity – Northwest School – **O** – Op Art – Orphism – Photorealism – Pixel Art – Plasticien – Plein Air – Pointillism – Pop Art – Post-impressionism – Precisionism – Pre-Raphaelitism – Primitivism – Process Art – Purism – **Q** – Qajar Art – **R** – Rasquache – Realism – Remodernism – Renaissance – Rococo – Romanesque – Romanticism – **S** – Samikshavad – Shin Hanga – Shock Art – Sōsaku Hanga – Socialist Realism – Sots Art – Space Art – Street Art – Stuckism – Suprematism – Surrealism – Symbolism – Synchromism – **T** – Tachisme – Toyism – Transgressive Art – **U** – Ukiyo-e – Underground commix – **V** – Vancouver School – Verdadism – Vorticism.

List of Art Materials and Techniques
A Animation | Assemblage (*Beads – Cardboard – Found Objects – Glue Paper – Textiles – Wire – Wood*) **C** Carving (*Granite – Ice – Ivory – Marble – Wood – Plaster – Stone – Wax*) Casting (*Aluminum – Bronze – Cement – Gold – Pewter – Plaster – Plastic – Silver – Synthetic Resin – Wax*) Ceramics | Cartooning | Comic Book **D** Design (*Advertising – Architecture – Fashion – Furniture – Graphic – Industrial – Interior – Jewelry – Production*) Drawing (*Chalk – Charcoal – Conté Crayon – Graphite – Ink – Marker – Pastel*) **F** Finishes (*Enamel – Patina – Polychrome – Wax*) **G** Graffiti **I** Illustration **M** Mixed Media | Modeling (Clay – Digital – Papier-Mâché – Plaster – Sand) **P** Painting (*Acrylic – Digital – Fingerpaint – Fresco – Gouache – Latex – Oil – Tempera – Watercolor*) Paper Cut | Photography (*Black & White – Color Tint – Film – Fisheye – Hand Coloured – Hipstamatic Hipstamatic – Infrared – Instagram – Polaroid – Sepia – Tilt-Shift*) Printing | Printmaking (*3D – Aquatint – Embossing – Engraving – Etching – Inkjet – Intaglio – Laser – Letterpress – Linocut – Lithography – Metalcut – Mezzotint – Moku Hanga – Monotype Relief – Etching – Screen – Styrofoam – Printing – Woodcut – Wood – Engraving*) **T** Tattooing.

HOW TO CHOOSE THE RIGHT FONT

Your choice of font can portray your style very quickly. Fonts can be very individualistic. There are many different types of fonts available, and most fonts fit into one of these categories: Serif, Sans Serif, Script, Blackletter, Titling, and Decorative, as shown in Figure 1.6.

Serif fonts have extensions from the ends of the character, which make the typefaces look more decorative and improves readability by adding a flow from one character to the next.

Sans Serif fonts are "without" serif ("Sans" means "without" in French). These typefaces are simple and clean.

Script fonts have derived from calligraphy and handwriting.

Blackletter fonts are very dense and the capitals are exceedingly decorated. They have developed from early liturgical writings and illuminated manuscripts.

Titling fonts are usually all capitals and look best at larger size.

Decorative fonts are more artistic, stylized, and eye-catching.

Serif
Sans Serif
Script
𝕭lackletter
TITLING
Decorative

Figure 1.6 Sample Fonts of Serif, Script, Blackletter, Titling, and Decorative

Without getting too technical or deep into the history of text and font, there are some basic vocabulary words that need to be understood and considered when it comes to text. See Figure 1.7.

The quick brown fox jumped over the lazy dog. The quick brown fox jumped over the lazy dog. The quick brown fox jumped over the lazy dog.

Figure 1.7 *The Character Window in Photoshop Allows the Adjustment of Kerning, Tracking, and Leading*

A **character** is an individual letter or symbol.

Spacing refers to the overall distance between two characters or words. Both characters and words should be well spaced (neither too close nor too far from other characters or words).

The quick brown fox jumped over the lazy dog. The quick brown fox jumped over the lazy dog. The quick brown fox jumped over the lazy dog.

Figure 1.8 *Characters Typed Using Default Spacing can be Adjusted Individually Using Kerning. This Image Specifically Looks at the Letters j u Before the Kerning Adjustment*

Kerning, as seen in Figure 1.8, refers to the space (more or less) in-between two characters. In order to get some typeface to be spaced evenly between some character combinations, you might need to adjust certain character pairs, instead of the entire word, as in Figure 1.9.

The quick brown fox jumped over the lazy dog. The
quick brown fox jumped over the lazy dog. The quick
brown fox jumped over the lazy dog.

Figure 1.9 *This Image Shows the Letters j u After the Kerning Adjustment*

Tracking refers to the space in-between all characters of a selected block of text, such as a word, sentence, or paragraph. Figure 1.10 shows the entire block of text after adjusting the tracking.

The quick brown fox jumped over the lazy dog. The
quick brown fox jumped over the lazy dog. The quick
brown fox jumped over the lazy dog.

Figure 1.10 *This Image Shows the Entire Block of Text After the Tracking Adjustment*

Leading refers to the vertical space in-between lines of text. This is also referred to as *Linc Spacing*. Leading usually needs to be adjusted, because the default is usually too far apart. Figure 1.11 shows the entire block of text after adjusting the leading.

Adjusting the spacing, kerning, tracking, and leading so that your text looks best is key. Don't just use the default settings dictate how your text will look.

You should limit your font choices to two but no more than three different types of font in your portfolio package. One font should be simpler and used for the majority of what you are writing. One or two other fonts can be used for highlighting certain words or using as headers. These fonts can

The quick brown fox jumped over the lazy dog. The quick brown fox jumped over the lazy dog. The quick brown fox jumped over the lazy dog.

Figure 1.11 *This Image Shows the Entire Block of Text After the Leading Adjustment*

be fancier and more fun than the other, but make sure they are very easy to read. Remember, legibility, and readability are the goals here. You want whoever is looking at your materials to be able to understand it without a lot of work. Swirly and fancy font choices can become difficult to decipher and a real strain on the eyes if it is used for too much text. I would suggest using complicated fonts sparingly, perhaps only in a logo design or for your name. Figure 1.12 shows some sample font options.

Font size also plays a part in readability. Make sure that you aren't using a font size that is too small to read. Print it out and ask anyone that you know who is over the age of 40 to read it. This is the age where eyesight tends to begin to weaken, and if they can't read it, make sure to increase your font size. Don't let your font take over or detract from the point of your design: promoting yourself and your abilities.

Make sure anything that you type has been looked at by other eyes to ensure that there are no typos or misspellings. If things are spelled wrong, it shows the studio or potential client that you do not pay enough attention to detail. Modeling is not spelled modelling. Plus, there is a big difference between a composter and a compositor. There is nothing worse than spending money on printing your business cards and letterhead only to find out that, when you receive them, something has been spelled wrong. It happens all the time.

When choosing a font for self-promotion, remember, you must consider who you are and how you want to be represented. Hopefully you have decided that at this point. What is your style? What adjectives did you choose to describe yourself?

Create contrast. This makes your design visually interesting. Creating visual contrast can create emphasis and make a strong impact on the viewer. You can do this by mixing typefaces, mixing font categories like Sans Serif and script, choosing a Serif and a Sans Serif, picking a much **heavier font** and lighter font, making some words larger and some smaller, making some words **bold** or *italicized*, and using all CAPITAL letters for some words and all lower case letters for others. If you choose to use all caps, do so sparingly, because all caps can be harder to read.

COLOR

COLOR THEORY

We can't think about color without a basic understanding of color theory. In the 1600s, Sir Isaac Newton was the first to prove that color comes from light, not objects, and that light can be refracted and reflected. From this developed two systems of light theory: additive and subtractive. The additive (refractive) system mixes or "adds" light waves to form colored light, and the "addition" of all light waves creates white light. The subtractive (reflected) system reflects the light waves that form the color of an object, and the object absorbs or "subtracts" the light waves that don't form the color of an object. The absorption of all light waves creates a black object, whereas the reflection of all light waves creates a white object. This is why it is a bad idea to own a black car and live in the Southeastern United States like I do. During the summer, the black car is extremely hot, because it is absorbing all of the light from the sun.

Apple Casual
Apple Chancery
Arial
Bauhaus 93
Book Antiqua
Calibri
Comic Sans MS
Monotype Corsiva
DESDEMONA
Edwardian Script ITC
Franklin Gothic Book
Georgia
Gill Sans Ultra Bold
Handwriting – Dakota
Helvetica
HERCULANUM
Hobo Std
Lucida Blackletter
Matura MT Script Capitals
Mistral
PERPETUA TITLING MT
ROSEWOOD STD
STENCIL STD
Tahoma
Zapfino

Figure 1.12 Some Sample Fonts

COLOR WHEEL

Before we discuss color harmony, we need to understand the color wheel. Color theory tells us that the primary colors for the subtractive system are RYB or red, yellow, and blue. The primary colors for the additive system are RGB or

If one says "red"—the name of color—and there are fifty people listening, it can be expected that there will be fifty reds in their minds. And one can be sure that all these reds will be very different.

Josef Albers

red, green, and blue. The definition of a primary color is a color that cannot be mixed from other colors. From these primary colors, we can *theoretically* mix every other color that exists. I have emphasized the word theoretically because mixing color with the subtractive system is not an exact science. There are many variables that can change the look of the resulting mixture, such as the type and quality of the pigment or paper. CMYK or cyan, magenta, yellow, and black is a second subtractive color model that was developed and perfected in the 19th century for printing, using the color separation process, when it was discovered through experiments that cyan, magenta, and yellow were the true subtractive primaries, not RYB. As a painter myself, I came to the realization several years ago that red and blue are not true reflective primaries, because red and blue can indeed be mixed from other combinations of colors, whereas cyan and magenta cannot. I can't help but make a comment here on how you cannot always believe what you were taught in school. After all, at some point in history, children were also taught that the world was flat.

The K in CMYK actually stands for "Key" and not black. The key plate was the first plate to be printed, and it was the black plate. Black ink was added into the printing process because of the limitations and expense of the colored inks. Mixing all three colors didn't really create black, but rather, more of a muddy brown, and was expensive to mix. Black ink provided a less-expensive solution that created darker blacks in the final print.

By mixing the primary colors together, we obtain the secondary colors. By mixing the secondary colors, we get tertiary colors. Table 1.1 lists the primary, secondary, and tertiary colors of all three color systems, RYB, CMYK, and RGB. Figure 1.13 shows the primary, secondary, and tertiary colors of all three color systems as they exist on a color wheel.

Table 1.1   *Color Chart*

	Subtractive Traditional Reflective	Subtractive True Reflective	Additive Refractive
Primary Colors	Red, Yellow, Blue	Cyan, Magenta, Yellow	Red, Green, Blue
Secondary Colors	Violet, Orange, Green	Blue, Red, Green	Yellow, Cyan, Magenta
Tertiary Colors	Red-Orange, Yellow-Orange, Yellow-Green, Blue-Green, Blue-Violet, Red-Violet	Cyan-Blue, Blue-Magenta, Red-Magenta, Orange, Yellow-Green, Cyan-Green	Orange, Yellow-Green, Cyan-Green, Cyan-Blue, Blue-Magenta, Red-Magenta

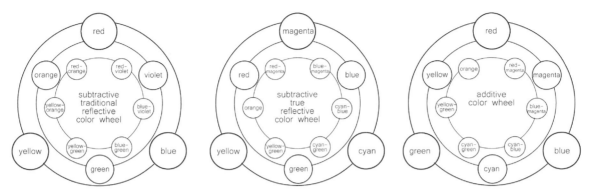

Figure 1.13 Subtractive and Additive Color Wheels

It is important to understand both the subtractive and the additive systems and realize that the color of red light looks differently if it is refracted or reflected. Why is this important? Because what you see on your computer monitor will probably not look the same once it is printed, and colors vary from monitor to monitor. The printed image is usually darker due to the quality of the inks or pigments and that of the paper, and because of the gamut range of a printed image is more limited than that of a computer monitor. The word gamut here refers to the complete range of intensity or subset of the color system when it is reproduced or output. As you are designing for pieces of your portfolio that will be viewed on both reflected (print) and refracted (computer monitor) systems, you must keep this information in front of your mind as you design. It's also a great idea to test print as you go so that you can make adjustments. You must also remember to work in CMYK for designing the print aspects of your package, or at the very least, convert the image from RGB to CMYK before sending it to the printer. You will notice that some of the colors become less intense on the monitor when switching from RGB to CMYK.

Colors are perceived differently by different people and are subject to change based on many circumstances:

- Reflected colors are affected by different light sources. For example, the same object will look differently inside, under fluorescent lighting, and outside, in sunlight. If the object is in sunlight, the time of day and conditions of the weather also affect the color perception of the object. Figure 1.14 shows both flourescent and incandescent lighting on the same bowl of oranges. A color version of this image can be found on www.reelsuccess.com
- Object colors are also affected by their surroundings. An object can be affected by light that has bounced off of other objects nearby. If a color is surrounded by another color, it is also perceived differently,

Figure 1.14 Reflected Colors Affected by Different Light Sources

as shown in Figure 1.15. A color version of this image can be found on www.reelsuccess.com. The exact same color, when surrounded by different adjacent colors, appears to have different values when compared visually side by side as it "interacts" with other colors.

Figure 1.15 Object Color Affected by Bounce Light

■ Refractive light, such as in the computer monitor or television, must be calibrated using a colorimeter for accuracy. If they are not, then the colors will differ from screen to screen. Calibrating a monitor will also give you a closer screen-to-print similarity.

ATTRIBUTES OF COLOR

Regardless of which color primary wheel you are working with, there are some basic facts and vocabulary that need to be remembered when working with color:

Hue is simply the name of the color: magenta, red, yellow, green, cyan, blue

Saturation | Chroma | Intensity are three words that synonymously refer to the pureness or brightness of a color. The use of bright, vivid, saturated colors draws attention and creates emphasis when paired with duller, less-saturated color.

Value is the lightness or darkness of the color. In order to create a focal point in your design, using highly contrasting colors (placing dark values next to light values) will cause the lighter values to leap forward visually. The lighter color can be used as an accent color in order to draw attention and create emphasis.

There is usually some confusion between saturation and value. How does lightness differ from brightness? Pure color equals brightest saturation. By adding white or black to a color, the value is changed, and at the same time the saturation becomes duller. By adding the same value gray, or the same value complimentary color, you would lose saturation without losing value. The color would then become less bright but not less dark. This means if both the pure color and the mixed color were converted to gray scale, they would be the same gray.

The following are color options available inside graphics software:

HSB in Photoshop or any other graphics software stands for hue, saturation, and brightness where hue is the color, and here, saturation is how much white is added to the color, and brightness is how much black is added. HSB is used to select a color, as well as RGB and CMYK options. The color # can be used to recreate that color in other software, such as recreating a color between Photoshop and Dreamweaver. The RGB values can also be used to recreate that color in other software, such as recreating a color between Photoshop and Maya. This sometimes requires changing the RGB scale from 0–1 to 0–255. Figure 1.16 shows the different HSB windows available in Photoshop. A color version of this image can be found on www.reelsuccess.com

HSL stands for hue, saturation, and lightness where hue is the color, saturation is how pure that color is in a range between pure color and removal of all color (which will give you a gray based on that color's value), and lightness is how much white or black is added in the value range. HSL is used to adjust the colors of an existing image. Figure 1.17 shows

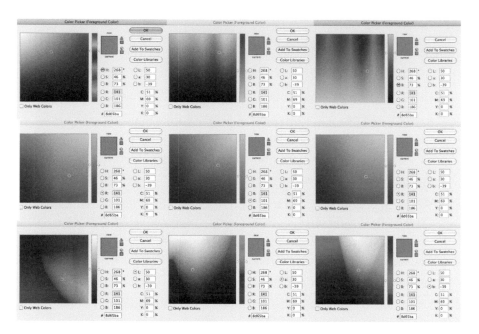

Figure 1.16 HSB Windows in Photoshop

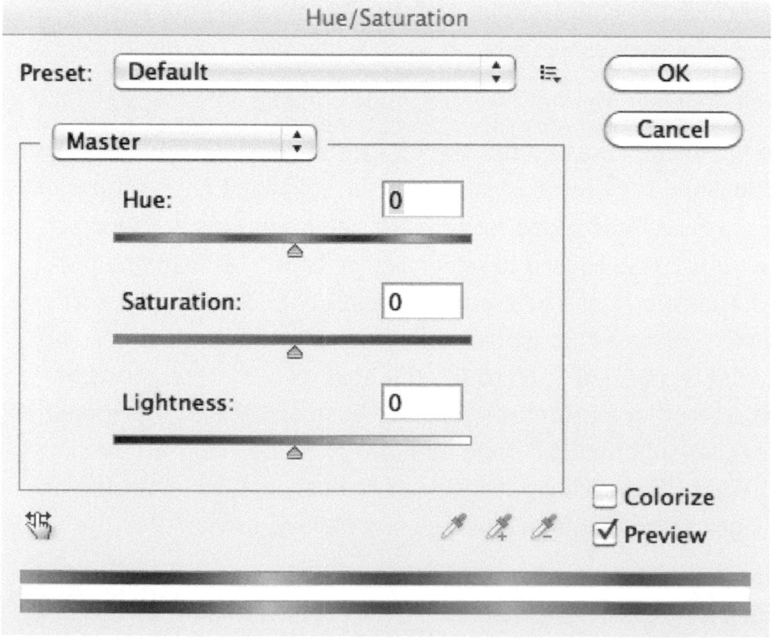

Figure 1.17 The HSL Window in Photoshop

the HSL window in Photoshop. A color version of this image can be found on www.reelsuccess.com

PSYCHOLOGICAL EFFECTS OF COLOR

Color has psychological effects on us that are very real. There have been studies done to show that certain colors affect people in predictable ways. For example, in 1979, Alexander G. Schauss, PhD, experimented with the use of the color pink and its effect on mood and behavior. After experimenting with various shades of pink, he found that a certain shade of pink (which he called Baker-Miller Pink, as seen in Figure 1.18. A color version of this image can be found on www.reelsuccess. com) decreased aggression approximately 30 minutes after the participants stared at the color for about 15 minutes. This color pink was utilized at Iowa State University in the 1970s as football coach Hayden Fry had the visiting team's locker room painted pink in an attempt to relax the players before heading onto the field. It has remained pink ever since. Color can also have physiological effects on humans. For example, red actually raises blood pressure and heart rate. This is why it is associated with both danger and love.

Baker-Miller Pink
Red:255 Green:145 Blue:175
hex: #FF91AF

Figure 1.18 Baker-Miller Pink RGB Values and Its Hexadecimal Color Code

Warm Versus Cool

We consider half of the color wheel to be "warm" and the other half to be "cool." Psychologically, we associate warmer colors with the heat of the day and cooler colors with coolness of the night. Magentas, reds, yellows, and oranges can actually physically "feel" warmer, whereas cyans, blues, greens, and purples "feel" cooler. Studies have actually proven that by painting a room "warm" or "cool" can affect the occupants inside that room accordingly.

Warm colors advance, and cool colors recede. High-contrast bright colors advance, and darker colors recede as well. By using this knowledge, you can use an accent color to "pop" a logo from the background or create emphasis and focus. An example business card, by Sean Buck using the warm and cool colors can be seen in Figure 1.19. A color version of this image can be found on www.reelsuccess.com

The Meaning of Color in Advertising

Don't forget that colors have meaning, and the meaning differs from culture to culture. You can use these meanings to help sell yourself, just as companies have been using marketing schemes that utilize

Figure 1.19 Warm Versus Cool Colors

this concept in their advertisements and brands. All colors have both positive and negative meanings attached to them.

Some common color associations:

Yellow: cowardly, sunny, cheerful, eye-catching

Orange: hot, playful, happy, childlike

Red: passionate, dangerous, excitement

Purple: contemplative, sensual, spiritual, regal, mystical

Blue: honest, dependable, sad, calm, tranquil

Green: new, earth-friendly, little experience, associations with money and prestige, nature, fresh

White: pure, clean, sterile, innocent

Grey: depressing, timeless, sophisticated, classic

Black: elegant, magical, mysterious

Brown: earthy, secure, rich

Following is a list of idioms and their meanings that are used in American culture, and from what I have found, many of them also hold true in other cultures as well.

Tickled pink	To be very pleased
The pink slip	Fired from a job
Seeing pink elephants	Had too much to drink
Rose-colored glasses	Looking at things unrealistically but in a more positive way
In the red	In debt
Take the red eye	Flying on a plane over night
Seeing red	Very angry
Caught red-handed	Guilty
That's a red flag	A feeling that something is wrong
Paint the town red	To go out and have a really good time
Red-carpet treatment	Being treated like a movie star
Yellow bellied	A coward
Green with envy	Jealous

Green-eyed monster	Jealousy
Green thumb	Being able to grow plants easily
Green	Very new to something
The green light	A signal to go ahead with a project
Feeling blue	Being sad
Talk until you are blue in the face	Repeating the same idea until you are out of breath
Once in a blue moon	Only on occasion
White lie	A lie that isn't really bad
True colors	To show the real you
Gray area	Not quite clear because it isn't black or white, it is somewhere in-between
Black sheep of the family	A family member who is the trouble maker or problem person
Born with a silver spoon in his mouth	A child of wealthy parents
In the dark	Not knowing what is going on
In the black	Making a profit
With flying colors	With great success
The black market	An illegal transaction
To blacklist someone	To exclude someone
To blackmail	To manipulate someone by threatening them
Black tie affair	An elegant occasion
It's either black or white	It is one way or the other
Carte Blanche	The freedom to do whatever you want
Wave the white flag	Surrender
Whitewash something	To cover up problems or mistakes

COLOR SCHEMES

You are advertising yourself and your work. Use color wisely. One rule of thumb is to create a limited palate and work only from those chosen colors and their range of values. Perhaps choose two or three colors, with one being an accent. Too many colors can be overwhelming and distract the viewer from the overall impact of your design. Here is where an understanding of color harmony and color schemes can be useful.

Colors must fit together as pieces in a puzzle or cogs in a wheel.

Hans Hofmann

Color harmony is simply the ability to choose colors that work well together. By sticking to the tried and true color schemes below, you can achieve color harmony successfully. You can also choose colors that don't work well together to create what is called **color discord**. Usually, this leaves the viewer with an unsettled feeling. It is risky to utilize clashing colors because of the message that can be visually perceived. This may backfire as you represent yourself as either someone who likes to "ruffle feathers" or as someone who does not know how to work with colors. Always keep in mind what your intention is for the viewer. Be mindful of every design choice. Figure 1.20 shows the following color harmonies, using red as a base color.

Monochromatic color schemes use only one color, or hue, and can include the changes in value by adding white or black.

Analogous color schemes use hues that are next to each other on a color wheel and can also include value changes.

Complementary color schemes use two colors that are located opposite to each other on the color wheel.

Split complementary color schemes use three colors; one color plus the two colors that lie adjacent to its complementary color.

Triadic color schemes use three colors that are equally spaced on a color wheel. The primary colors are an example of a triadic color scheme.

> Color can overwhelm....one must understand that when it comes to color, "less" is often "more"— lesson taught us by the masters but ignored by many artists.
>
> Joe Singer

If you're not good with color, stick with something that already works. Choose one of your best pieces and pull the colors from there. What if your work doesn't involve the use of color (you are a rigger perhaps)? Find one of your favorite paintings by your favorite artist and choose colors that come out of that work. Find your favorite shirt or fabric and use the colors that you find there. Look around. Color is everywhere. Think about the colors used in the products you consume on a daily basis, the restaurants and stores you frequently visit, and the packaging of the items you purchase. Look at the color schemes in nature. Limit yourself to two or three colors. Be very careful when choosing colors for fonts. Color and value can sometimes make the font more difficult to read.

Adobe has this great website and mobile app that will help you generate color themes. There are also existing themes that you can browse through (http://kuler.adobe.com/).

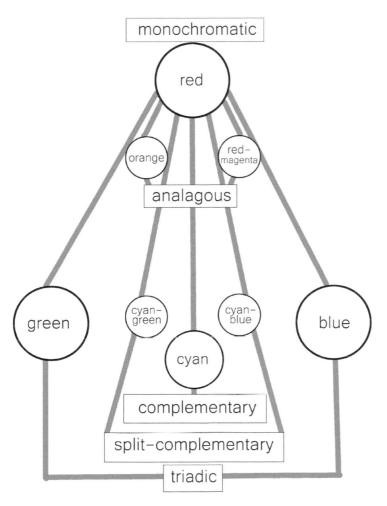

Figure 1.20 Color Harmonies Where Red Is the Base Color

If you want to learn more about color theory, there are several sources listed at the end of this chapter. As this book is in black and white, color examples can be found on the companion website at www.reelsuccess.com.

COMPOSITION OF DESIGN

The Merriam-Webster dictionary defines composition as the act or process of composing; specifically arrangement into specific proportion or relation and especially into artistic form. Composition of design is a thoughtful process. You want to be able to catch someone's eye and deliver a message in an

> Composition is the art of arranging in a decorative manner the various elements which the painter uses to express his sentiments. In a picture every separate part will be visible and ... everything which has no utility in the picture is for that reason harmful.
>
> Henri Matisse

> Before you compose your picture it's a good idea to ask yourself why you're doing it.
>
> Anonymous

> Composing a picture, do many thumbnails, rejecting the obvious ones.
>
> Irwin Greenberg

esthetically intriguing or pleasing way. In self-promotion, the message you are delivering is you.

Form and function are important for design. Be cautious not to spend all your time making your design beautiful and artistically intriguing that you forget the reason it needs to be useful. You want people to contact you. Don't make them work to find your contact information. Make this information easy to find. While this seems like perfect common sense, I can assure you that many nondesigners and designers alike forget to put function in the forefront of their design. When designing, do not forget about the minimalistic approach. Too much clutter confuses the viewer and makes information hard to find. It is perfectly fine to use white space as a way to cause the viewer to focus on what is important.

When you begin designing any composition, begin by drawing thumbnails of as many ideas as possible. Never settle for your first idea. Research what other designers have done. Once you have several ideas, take each idea and develop about 10 different variations.

The following are some universal compositional rules that should be implemented to ensure a strong design. Utilize at least one of these rules when composing your design.

THE GOLDEN MEAN

Pythagoras was the father of math and music. He observed certain patterns and numbers reoccurring in nature. Pythagoras believed that beauty was associated with the ratio of small integers. He discovered that the pentagram diagonals, when cut apart into sections, created the proportions of the Golden Section when two sections were combined together (one section plus then next larger section) as seen in Figure 1.21. The Golden Section had the Golden Ratio of 1:1.6180339887. . .

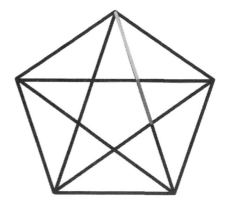

Figure 1.21 The Golden Section Derived from a Pentagon

Inside the pentagram were also the proportions of the Golden Rectangle, which is created by opening the sides of the hidden triangular shape of the pentagram, as seen in Figure 1.22.

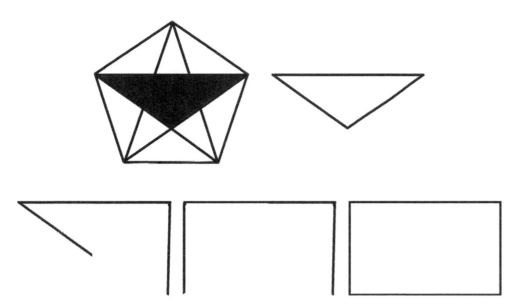

Figure 1.22 The Golden Rectangle

The Golden Rectangle can mathematically reproduce itself indefinitely by dividing the rectangle using the Golden Section proportions into both an internal square and another Golden Rectangle, as seen in Figure 1.23.

Drawing a quarter circle in each square of the segmented Golden Rectangle forms a Golden Spiral, as seen in Figure 1.24.

The Golden Section, Golden Rectangle, and Golden Spiral can be found throughout nature. The Greeks considered the Golden Rectangle as the mathematical basis for beauty and architecture. The Golden Rectangle is a universal rule used in design and art because the proportions are pleasing to the eye.

You can find a downloadable Golden Rectangle and Golden Spiral overlay to use when designing on www.reelsuccess.com.

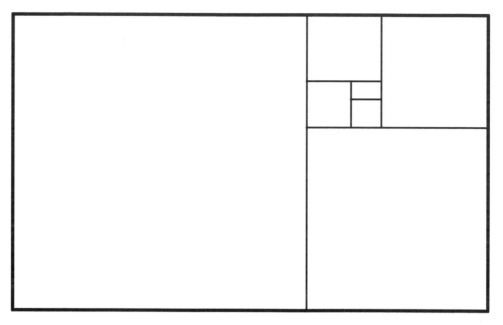

Figure 1.23 *The Golden Rectangle with Internal Divisions*

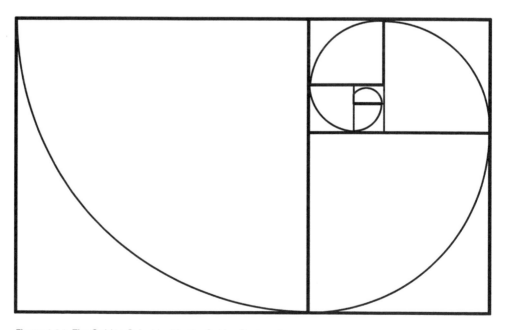

Figure 1.24 *The Golden Spiral Inside the Golden Rectangle*

THE RULE OF THIRDS

The rule of thirds is a compositional guideline that can be considered as a simplified version of the Golden Rectangle, as seen in Figure 1.25. The major difference is that this rule can be used on any proportioned composition, whether it is a rectangle, square, circle, and so forth. The rule of thirds states that dividing a composition into nine equal parts using two equally spaced horizontal and vertical lines can create a visual interesting composition by placing important compositional elements along these lines or at the point of their intersection.

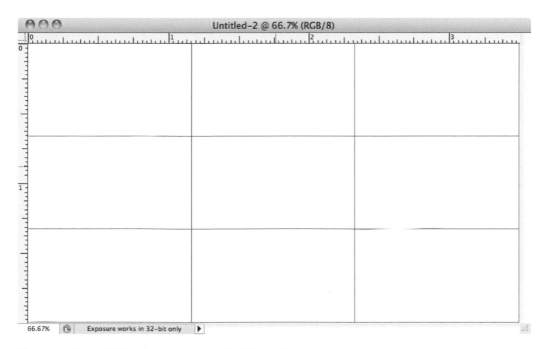

Figure 1.25 Rule of Thirds Grid for Business Card Dimensions

For overlaying a rule of thirds grid automatically for all work in Photoshop, all that needs to be done is to set the grid preferences and view the resulting grid. To set grid preferences on a mac, as seen in Figure 1.26:

1. From the Photoshop menu, select Preferences, then Guides, Grids, and Slices.
2. In the Preferences dialogue box, set the Grid Line to **33.33 percent** and the subdivisions to **1**.
3. You can also choose a more prominent color, like red, instead of gray.
4. Click **OK**.
5. From the **View** menu, select **Show>Grid**.

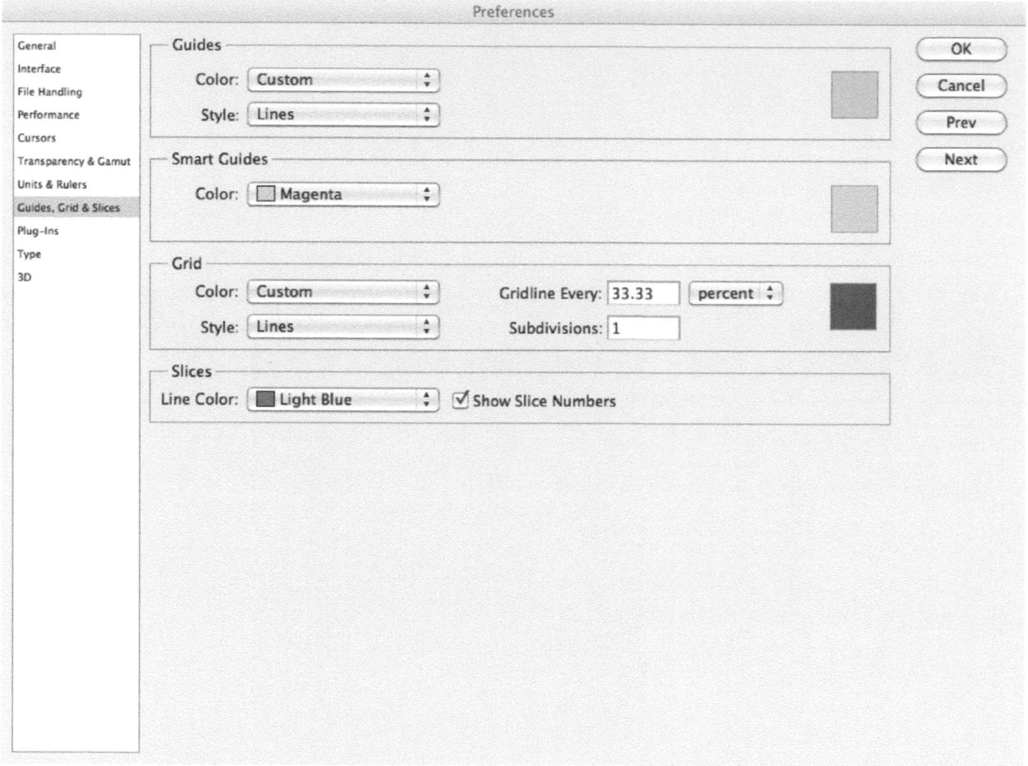

Figure 1.26 Photoshop Dialogue Box

GEOMETRICAL SHAPES

Geometrical shapes can also be used to create unified compositions and can help create movement by directing the viewer's eye across the surface. Important elements can be placed in a composition to create diagonals, S-curves, circles, and triangles. The triangular composition is probably the most recognized and used throughout art and design history.

PERSONAL PROMOTION

You must become your own personal promoter, unless you have the money to hire a professional artist representative. Hiring a representative will free up your time as a creative. An artist rep is different from an agent. Although agent representation is more common for writers and storytellers, other creative types will have a much more difficult time finding an agent, who helps their clients look for work and negotiate contracts.

A professional artist representative is someone who can help you get noticed. There are several agencies out there that are geared toward specific areas of art, such as illustration. Some of these agencies will help represent animation creatives. They usually have a website that lists the talent and the portfolios of the artists that they represent. The benefit of using a representative is networking. Their website becomes a "one stop shopping" location for anyone looking for artists. Chapter 7 goes into much more detail about the benefits and "how to's" of networking.

But really, the best thing you can do is become your own promoter or team up with a few friends and work together by promoting one another. So, once you have your professional package together, be sure to read through Chapter 7 and see how to get your name out there.

Recommended Reading List

Design Workshop by Robin Williams

Type Rules! by Ilene Strizver

Graphically Speaking by Lisa Buchannan

Design Basics by David Lauer and Stephen Pentack

Pantone Guide to Communicating with Color by Leatrice Eiseman

Interaction of Color by Josef Albers

Adobe Type Library Reference Book by Adobe Systems, Inc.

BASIC DESIGN RULES

DO's AND DON'Ts

- Direct the eye, don't over clutter your design.
- Be aware of space. Look at the negative space.
- Don't place images or text too close to the edges of anything.
- You may conscientiously overlap objects, but if overlapping text, be sure that the text is still readable.
- Don't choose colors or fonts that make reading difficult.
- Colors that are too close in value are difficult to read when placed on top of each other.
- Use no more than two or three different fonts.
- Limit your colors to two or three.

- Make sure that everything is legible.
- Make sure that the design is functional. Will people know who you are and how to contact you?

ACTION LIST

BRAINSTORMING

- Define who you are or how you want to present yourself using adjectives.
- Choose two or three of your best pieces.
- Create a list of objects that represent who you are.
- Identify two or three of your favorite artists.
- Establish your favorite two or three art movements.
- Identify five or ten fonts that strike your interest.
- Choose a color theme. Begin with your favorite colors.

CREATING

- Collect images of different textures or patterns that reflect your interests.
- Collect 30–50 images that reflect your choices of adjectives, objects, artists, art movements, and colors. This can include images you have already collected, like your artwork.
- Design a logo or develop your identity: a theme or "look."
- Draw 30 thumbnails of different ideas. Start with the first ideas that come to mind. Try to come up with five completely different ideas. From these ideas, develop each one in six different ways. Our creative brains do amazing things when pushed to the limit, so do not settle for the first idea that pops into your head. Thoroughly explore various options.
- From the thumbnails, narrow the ideas down to two or three. The layout process can begin once you have decided on a logo or look, or have narrowed it down to a couple of ideas. If designing a logo, remember that a good logo should be easily recognizable, and it should be easy to recognize on both a business card or a billboard.

NOTE

1   This word bank is from a book entitled *Graphically Speaking* by Lisa Buchanan, with my additions.

CHAPTER 2

PROFESSIONAL PACKAGE PRESENTATION

THE PACKAGE: CONTENTS

Creating a beautifully designed portfolio package looks professional. People will know that you take your work seriously. However, it is important to know that no matter how professionally you package your work, if your work isn't good, then you have wasted your time creating the package. So first, spend your time developing the content of your portfolio; then, and only then, package and promote your work.

The contents of your professional package should contain the following: a business card, a cover letter, résumé, demo reel or portfolio, breakdown list, and web presence. It could also contain, if required by the company, a reel submission form and DVD label and case. Some companies only accept applications through e-mail or website and explicitly say that they absolutely do not accept mailed submissions. You should design all these pieces together, so that they form a cohesive package. In this chapter, we take a look at each of these items in detail.

Most of these information should be present online. The rest can be printed on an as needed basis, dependent on the individual requirements of each company's application process. A demo reel showcases your very best work, a cover letter is written specifically for each job for which you are applying, a résumé is tailored to show that you have the necessary qualifications listed in the job description, a breakdown list accompanies the demo reel with specific information regarding each clip seen on the reel, and web presence is necessary so that your information is easily accessible, whether it be a full website or simply a blog where your work can be seen. A reel submission form gives a company permission to view your work while it releases them from any prosecution or liability for any similarity found in relation to their current or future work and, if required, is usually downloadable from the individual company requesting one.

Examples for each element will be presented in this chapter. Additional examples can be found on the website www.reelsuccess.com.

LOGO, IDENTITY, OR BRAND

All your materials should be unified by a design that represents you. This could be a logo that you've designed to brand yourself or simply a color scheme that is carried throughout all of your presentation materials.

One of the things that you do not want to do is to market yourself as a company, unless you are actually creating your own company as in Figure 2.1.

Figure 2.1 *An Example Business Card of Someone Who, with Two Other Friends, Started Their Own Studio*

Major production studios want to see you as the artist who is applying for the position. They are not looking to hire another company, but rather a person to fill a specific position. So market yourself as an individual artist.

You also want to consider the fact that over time your name can change, and how that name change affects your identity. For example, my given name and surname is Cheryl Cookmeyer. I was married in my 20s and became Cheryl Fell. I developed my original "logo" using my initials CF as shown in Figure 2.2.

Figure 2.2 *My Original Logo Business Card*

Then I divorced and married again in my 30s and became Cheryl Cabrera. I then changed from a logo to a more streamlined look I had developed from some video footage and After Effects, as shown in Figure 2.3.

Figure 2.3 My Current Business Card

Professionally, I am now known as Cheryl Cabrera. But with a recent divorce, I am now questioning what to do with my name, should I keep it professionally, or should I change it. Changing my name (now that I am established professionally) may cause confusion, but it also advertises my personal status to the world. So as you develop your professional identity, regardless of your situation, you should consider all possibilities and follow through with what option works best for you.

If you have not yet done so, complete the Action List at the end of Chapter 1, which will help you come up with a logo or an idea for a visual theme that ties your materials together.

BUSINESS CARD/NETWORKING CARD

The purpose of a business card is to provide someone with the information they need to contact you. This should be the most important aspect of the card. Basic information, such as your name, phone number, and e-mail address, is all that is really needed. You can also include a mailing address. If the person has a difficult time reading the card, they may become irritated or simply not even bother with you at all. Remember that most of the people looking at this card are probably going to be over the age of 40, so you really want to make sure that the font size is not too small in case they are farsighted.

A business card is 2 × 3½ inches. Don't be tempted to design an odd-shaped or -sized card because they usually create more problems than they are worth. When designing your business cards, you must consider the bleed while printing and usually add an additional 1/8 inch border making the total dimensions 2¼ × 3¾ inches. A bleed is necessary so that when the cards are cut, there is no chance of a hairline error, or in other words, a sliver of white paper showing between your graphic and the edge of the card after the machine cuts the cards. Extending a graphic or color beyond the actual dimensions of the card

bleed 1/8 inch = bleed 0.125 inches = bleed 0.3175 centimeters
safe zone 1/8 inch = safe zone 0.125 inches = safe zone 0.3175 centimeters

Figure 2.4 My Current Business Card Showing the Safe Zone and Bleed Areas

allows for some wiggle room and margin of error. You also need to allow for an inside 1/8 inch border for a safe zone for the same reason. You wouldn't want something important trimmed off, like the last digit of your phone number. Figure 2.4 shows my current business card with the safe zone and bleed areas. Always check with the printing company that you are using, because they may have different requirements.

If printing business cards at home, do so only on a laser printer. If the card is printed on an inkjet printer and gets wet, you will have a blurred mess in your hands. Also, do not print on those perforated business card sheets. Nothing screams amateur more than handing out perforated business cards. Print on solid cardstock and use an x-acto knife or paper cutter. Make sure your cards are square and cut precisely. If you have trouble with precision cuts, you should really consider getting them printed by a professional.

www.overnightprints.com and www.pressexprint.com are two online printers that I have personally used and have received a great quality product.

The business card should have a color scheme that allows the person receiving it a place to jot down notes about you, so that they can remember where and when they met you. This is incredibly important when at networking events, such as conferences or festivals, because one person can gather so many cards, they may have a difficult time remembering in what context they received your card. This is why a black business card on both sides is generally a bad idea. Although stylistically it may be appealing, functionally the card becomes somewhat useless.

Today, networking cards are becoming popular, where people list their social media information like Facebook or Twitter. I would caution you against this unless you want prospective employers or clients reading your mindless ramblings or seeing that photo where you were tagged while you posed half-naked and drunk. More on this will be considered in Chapter 4 when we get into the discussion about social media.

Sample business card designs, Figures 2.5 through 2.11:

Figure 2.5 *Sample Business Card Design by Philip Negroski*

Figure 2.6 *Bridget Kieffer*

Figure 2.7 *Sample Business Card Design by Ashley DeMattos*

Figure 2.8 *Sample Business Card Design by Juan Rivera*

Figure 2.9 *Sample Business Card Design by Melissa Massingill*

RANDY STRATTON
CHARACTER ANIMATOR

1139 MARIBOB CIRCLE
SAVANNAH, GEORGIA 31406

MORPHEOUS_S@YAHOO.COM

Figure 2.10 Sample Business Card Design by Marcos Carrasco

LETTERHEAD

Letterhead is designed stationery with a heading that consists of a name and contact information, along with your logo or identity design, and something that you should probably take some time in developing. It provides a professional representation of what you normally would use while printing correspondence on plain paper. It's also good idea to make a digital letterhead image that can be used on the top of documents and PDF files. I don't recommend embedding the image into an e-mail, because your e-mail may be considered spam with this as an attachment and filtered into the intended receiver's spam folder.

Letterhead should be designed in two parts. First, there is a main page graphic and layout for all single-page correspondence and the first page of multipage correspondence and is printed A4 in size, or 8½ × 11 inches (210 × 297 mm). This page should contain your logo or look, your mailing address, and contact phone numbers. Your mailing address is pertinent here, because letterhead is generally used for printed correspondence. E-mail and URL can also be listed. Second, there is a page layout for any additional pages of correspondence. The second page generally only minimally continues the theme of the first page.

If you have the money to have your letterhead professionally printed, then also include a design for an envelope and have that printed, too. Generally speaking, however, designing a label to use on envelopes or packages is sufficient and more cost-effective. Your letterhead, envelopes, and labels should have a similar layout as that of your business card. Doing so produces a cohesive and unified professional presentation.

Sample letterhead designs, Figures 2.11 through 2.14:

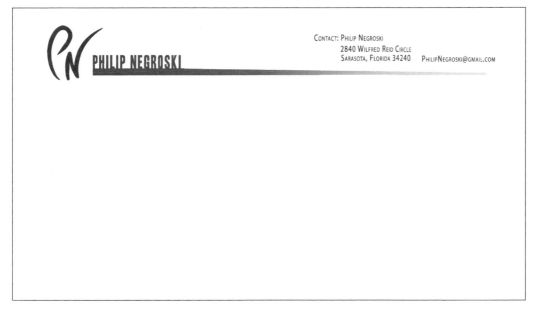

Figure 2.11 Sample Letterhead Design by Philip Negroski

Figure 2.12 Sample Letterhead Design by Bridget Kieffer

Ashley DeMattos
Animator · Illustrator

aludemattos@gmail.com   ashlimations.blogspot.com

Figure 2.13 Sample Letterhead Design by Ashley DeMattos

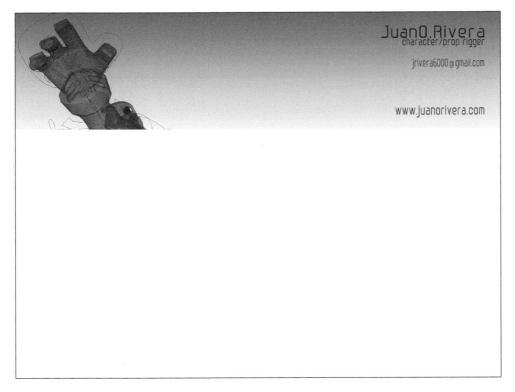

Figure 2.14 Sample Letterhead Design by Juan Rivera

COVER LETTER

Every cover letter that you send out should be tailored for each position and application. A cover letter is where you introduce yourself to the company that you're applying. It is not a place to repeat what is on your résumé. Keep your cover letter brief. A cover letter should definitely be no more than one page.

When addressing the cover letter, it is much better to address it to someone who actually works at the company instead of "to whom it may concern." This is where networking and research come into play. If you know someone at the company, it's best to address your cover letter to them and ask them to pass it on to the appropriate person. If you don't know someone at the company, you can find someone who works in the human resource department and address it to that person. Be careful; because recruiters move around from company to company, make sure that your connection is still actually working there. Usually someone in human resources will be the first one to look over your materials.

In the first paragraph, make sure to include the information on where you have found the job listing. The job listing could have been found on the Internet at a particular website, or you could have heard of the opening by word of mouth from someone you know. If this is the case and you are addressing the letter to the same person, you could start letter with something like, "I am applying for the position that you told me about."

The main body of the cover letter should explain that you have the qualifications that they are looking for and utilize the exact wording that is found in the job description. You should talk about how you can be an asset to their company. You have to convince them that they absolutely need you. It is not the place to tell them how they are going to help you with your career. Companies know that they can help develop you as an artist, animator, compositor, or whatever. You don't have to tell them what you will get from them. However, you must convince them that you are the person whom they have been looking for to fill the position. Tell them what you can bring to their company that no one else can. Tell them how you differ from the rest.

Sample Cover Letters, Figures 2.15 through 2.20:

Please consider me as an applicant for a compositing or digital artist position on your staff. I am currently completing my M.F.A. in Computer Art at the Savannah College of Art and Design. This achievement, combined with my background in art and theater, has prepared me to be a valuable asset to your company. My professional experience establishes my history of responsibility, commitment, and diversity.

During both of my internships, I had the opportunity to help develop creative ideas, work with clients, and complete projects. I chose to complete a second internship at a smaller company to further my experiences and to learn about the business of animation.

Prior to graduate school, I taught high school Art for four years and began a computer art program at that school. I am also an exhibiting painter currently represented by a gallery in New Orleans. Being able to successfully juggle school, work, and exhibitions has proven to me that I work efficiently under pressure. I excel at multitasking as well as tackling new concepts and projects. Through my wide range of experiences, I have proven to be successful both as a leader and a team player.

I consider myself an artist and a designer first. My experiences and studies have confirmed the importance of a traditional foundation. A strong foundation shows through my work, regardless of the medium.

I am enclosing my resume and reel for your review. I would like to meet with you to discuss opportunities with your company. I know I would be a valuable addition to your team. I look forward to hearing from you. Thank you for your time and consideration.

Figure 2.15 Sample Cover Letters

The Big University
1234 Big Street
Tinsel Town, CA 12345

Dear Mr. Jones,

Please consider me as an applicant for the Professor of Visual Effects - Procedural 3-D position in the School of Film and Digital Media at the Savannah College of Art and Design. I have learned of this position on your College's website.

With an M.F.A. in Visual Effects from the Savannah College of Art and Design combined with my background in Systems Administration at the college, I am prepared to be a valuable asset. During my Teaching Assistantship, I had much to offer and developed a great rapport with the students. I would be honored to contribute my talents and energy into the mission of the college and help prepare talented students for careers in Film and Digital Media. My previous professional experience establishes my history of responsibility, commitment, and diversity.

Teaching courses in Houdini would be my main area of interest. However, I would also be willing to teach other Visual Effects courses and sections of CMPA 100 or 110.

Enclosed is my resume and reel for your review. Please feel free to contact me to schedule a time to meet and discuss opportunities with your college. I know I would be an important addition to your faculty. I look forward to hearing from you. Thank you for your time and consideration.

Sincerely,

First Lastname

Figure 2.16 Sample Cover Letters

Ms. Martini:

I was very pleased when I came across an advertisement for an employment opportunity with School Zone Interactive. I have long been interested in working as an animator for School Zone, and have been watching for openings. I am very excited about this opportunity!

I would like to take this chance to offer you some preliminary information about my qualifications. I am currently pursuing an MFA in Animation from the Savannah College of Art and Design and have graduated from Grand Valley State University with a double major in Art and Design and Film and Video, animation emphasis.

Through my education and other experiences, I have developed many qualities that will make me an asset to your team. As my resume indicates, I worked as an animator for Animated Presentations for Education, creating interactive educational animations for use in undergraduate scientific study. During this experience I worked quickly to finish all projects within a set amount of work hours. I proved I am capable of taking direction from a client, problem solving creatively, and designing for a target audience. I also have experience working in a collaborative environment to create a short film, and I also participated in the 2005 Kalamazoo Animation Festival International's Cartoon Challenge. An intense four-day animation competition, the Cartoon Challenge has improved my skills of collaboration. During this competition, I feel I proved my ability to work under intense pressure, collaborate with other team members, and handle deadlines.

I would love to present my portfolio in person as well as answer any questions you may have about my skills and experiences. Please feel free to call me or contact me through email, if you have any questions or comments for me. Thank you very much for your time and cooperation.

Sincerely,

Figure 2.17 Sample Cover Letters

Pixar Animation Studios
1200 Park Avenue
Emeryville, California 94608
Telephone: 510 922-3000

Position: Internship for Art or story

Dear Sir/Madam,

An internship is the final requirement necessary to complete my M.F.A. in animation at the Savannah College of Art and Design. I am very pleased to apply the internship with Pixar. I am interested in either the Art or Story Internship position. As a pioneer of 3D animation, Pixar always displays fire-new ideas and impressions to the world. I am fascinated with the aesthetic and creativity in every feature film. I am looking forward to gain the professional knowledge about the design process and production pipeline, and I believe my background and experience will help me be an asset to your company in a very short time.

To be a concept designer and storyboard artist has always been my dream. I have a passion for creating and exploring my imagination through multimedia, such as traditional drawing, digital 3D, sculpture, and even stop motion animation. In addition, based on my theatre design background, I believe that "life" offers every essential element to characters and stories so that the performance can be thoughtful and impressed. I like to watch people, observe what they do, and apply what I see to my peculiar design. Furthermore, I have good sense about camera movement and layout. The process of previsualization attracts me as well as concept design. I have not only strong drawing skills but also Maya modeling and texturing techniques, and I am conscientious about meeting deadlines with a strong work ethic. My ultimate goal is to see my design performing on the big screen.

This portfolio package includes my resume, DVD reel, flatbook, and a link to my website. I am really interested in becoming a part of this internship and appreciate that you offer this opportunity for sending my portfolio to such an outstanding company.

Thank you for your initial interest.

Sincerely,

Figure 2.18 Sample Cover Letters

Dear Blue Sky Intern Coordinator,

My name is Philip Negroski and I am submitting my application to be considered for your animation internship spot.

I wholeheartedly believe that Blue Sky has the facility and the team to help me cultivate and focus my passion, skills, dedication, leadership and teamwork to create incredibly realistic, unique, and emotive animation. I push myself to be a value to any team and will continue to learn and expand in my discipline as a character animator, and to explore and understand other skills relating to the production so that they will benefit my discipline.

Being able to work alongside Blue Sky's team of talented and diverse animators would be an incredible and unforgettable opportunity.

Along with this cover letter, I have included my resume, recommendation letters, breakdown sheet, and a DVD with my demo reel. At your discretion, I have also included the "Flower Story" short film on the DVD.

Thank you for your consideration!

- Philip Negroski

Figure 2.19 Sample Cover Letters

Dear Intern Coordinator

I recently read about the Production Management summer internship at Blue Sky Studios on your company website. I have always been interested in your company because of the entertaining stories and high quality animation it produces. After visiting the studio this past December, there is no studio I would rather work for! I would appreciate the opportunity to be considered for a position in the summer internship program at your innovative company.

I have recently graduated with a BA in Digital Media: Visual Language from the University of Central Florida. Visual Language is a specialized program that mirrors the animation production pipeline used in the industry. My class of 26 students was given the opportunity to produce two animated short films our senior year. This allowed me to learn and work on all aspects of the animation production pipeline while working in a team environment.

I was always passionate about film, but I instantly fell in love with the overall animation production process. My primary task on my group's film was production manager and Lead Animator. I have always been a diligent, hardworking person, but throughout this experience I have learned how to maintain a consistently good work ethic, how to improve my multitasking and organizational skills, and how to work with others to achieve a common goal. I would like to be given the opportunity to showcase these skills by being accepted into your internship program.

I have included my resume and a short essay, which contain additional information about my qualifications and experience. I look forward to hearing from you. Thank you for your consideration.

Sincerely,

Figure 2.20 Sample Cover Letters

RÉSUMÉ/CURRICULUM VITAE

Your résumé lists all the information that shows you have the qualifications that meet the job description to which you are applying and should be tailored to each position to which you apply. An entry-level résumé should be no longer than one page. A seasoned professional should keep their résumé no longer than two pages. The résumé should be created digitally, with links where appropriate to validate the information you provide. The printed résumé should contain the URLs. There are different categories that can be listed on a résumé, but you must always have the following: education, experience, and skills. Always list the content in reversed chronological order, starting with your most recent accomplishments.

A curriculum vitae or CV is similar to a résumé, but it has more of an academic focus. It includes education, experience, and skills just as the résumé, but it also contains other information about experiences divided into three categories: research and creative endeavors, teaching, and service to the industry. Most CVs are lengthy, as they are very detailed. Employers in Europe, the Middle East, Africa, and Asia usually expect to receive a CV from an applicant, whereas in the United States, a CV is used when applying for academic or research positions and for fellowship or grant applications.

Always list your qualifications in the order as stated in the job description for which you are applying. Make your information easy to find and easy for whomever is looking at your résumé or CV to see that your qualifications meet those in the job description. As part of countless search and hiring committees, I have experience trying to sift through applicants' résumé pages trying to find the minimum qualifications needed. It is extremely frustrating and time consuming.

Some of the common categories found on creative résumés are as follows:

Header: Contact information including name, mailing address, phone number, e-mail address, and URL

Objective | Profile | Summary: There are arguments that an objective statement is not necessary, because they repeat information already in the cover letter. In addition, they tell the company what you want, and well, quite frankly, employers already know what you want since you applied for the position. Instead of using an objective statement, a profile or summary can be used. Talk about who you are and what sets you apart and above from the other applicants. The profile or summary should be tailored to each position and company and for each job application.

Education: Education information should include where and when any degrees were earned. No high school information should be listed here or anywhere else on your résumé.

Certification or Specialized Training: In addition to education, any specialized training or certification should be listed.

Professional Experience: Experience related to the job you are applying for should include companies where you have worked and a short description of what you did while you worked there. If you are a graduating student without experience in the field, you can list relevant coursework here. Describe briefly what the courses covered and what experience you received from the specific projects that you completed.

Work Experience: Any other work experience that you have can be listed here, especially if you can show that you have worked while you went to school.

Technology Skills: The types of tools that you use (including hardware and software, programming languages, and operating systems) should also be listed. Separating these items into two categories, familiarity and proficiency, is a really good idea. You can also include the number of years that you have used each tool.

Exhibitions and Festival Screenings: Have you created independent films and had them accepted into festivals? Has your artwork been displayed in galleries or museums? If so, list when and where, and if any awards were won.

Honors and Awards: List any academic or professional accolades.

Professional Organizations: List any that you belong to, such as SIGGRAPH, Women in Animation, ASIFA, Society for Animation Studies, and so on.

Conferences/Workshops: List and indicate if you attended or presented, along with the name of the conference, date, and location.

Sample Résumé:

3606 PENINSULA CIRCLE
MELBOURNE, FL 32940

E-MAIL: BRIDGET.KIEFFER@GMAIL.COM
BRIDGETKIEFFER.BLOGSPOT.COM

OBJECTIVE

To obtain an internship or full time job in production management.

EDUCATION

University of Central Florida	Orlando, FL	2007 – present

– BA in Digital Media: Visual Language, Graduation: May 2012
– Minor in Mass Communications
– GPA: 3.87

RELEVANT EXPERIENCE

Box Forts	University of Central Florida	Undergraduate short film project 2011 – 2012

– Served as Production Manager and Lead Animator on a five minute animated short film, working with a team of 12 other students.
– Rigged one of the characters.
– Composited multiple scenes in Nuke.

QUALIFICATIONS

– Proficient in Maya, Photoshop, Word, PowerPoint
– Familiar with Nuke, Premiere Pro, Final Cut Pro, Shake, Excel
– Worked in both Mac and Windows platforms.
– Ability to work effectively in team environment as well as independently.
– Ability to learn new skills quickly.

OTHER EXPERIENCE

DRS Technologies	Melbourne, Fl	2009 Summer Internship

– Prepared materials and video taped training sessions for the Professional Development Program (PDP).
– Updated and maintained the SharePoint site for the Training Department.
– Reviewed resumes, organized and planned intern events for the Recruiting Department.
– Entered and updated employee information in the Automatic Data Processing (ADP) system for Human Resources.

DRS Technologies	Melbourne, Fl	2008 Summer Internship

– Created marketing product datasheets using Quark software.
– Prepared product proposals by editing text and images using Microsoft PowerPoint and Word.
– Prepared PowerPoint presentations for Business Development group.

Figure 2.21 Sample Résumé by Bridget Kieffer

MATTSCOTTJUSTICE@GMAIL.COM
WWW.MATTSCOTTJUSTICE.COM
954.415.4616

Profile

I wish to work in an environment that allows me to learn and grow as an artist along with allowing me to gain experience to one day become a leader in the industry. I value work ethic greatly along with always improving my artistic talent. I have an open mind that is ready to learn. I strive to be as creative as possible and never give up when a problem arises.

Skills

• Maya - Modeling, Textures, Shaders, Effects, Animation, Layout, Rendering
• Photoshop - Matte Painting, Texture Painting, Graphic work
• Illustrator - Logos, Vector Graphics
• Mudbox - 3d Sculpting, 3d Painting
• Nuke / Shake - Compositing effects, layering footage, color correction
• Final Cut Pro - Editing

Experience

3D ARTIST INTERN, GEOMOTION GROUP, ORLANDO FLORIDA — 2012
Produced 3d environments to be used in exercise DVDs for kids. Modeled, textured, rendered environments.

MODELER, SENIOR PRODUCTION, UCF, ORLANDO, FLORIDA — 2011-2012
Modeled various props for senior production. Modeled Character for senior production. Props modeled include: trees, bus, houses, sputnik, cardboard boxes.

ART DIRECTOR, SENIOR PRODUCTION, UCF, ORLANDO, FLORIDA — 2010-2012
Designed and developed the visual style of the film. Responsible for designing most the assets and seeing them through to modeling. Critiqued peers work and make sure it is on style. Responsible for producing the color script of our film and organizing others to work on it. Created various style guides and reference pages for people to refer to.

TEXTURE LEAD, SENIOR PRODUCTION, UCF, ORLANDO, FLORIDA — 2011-2012
Went through all the assets and made lists of all the textures needed and assigned people to them. Set deadlines for critiques and final revisions. Textured the two main characters of our film and set up shaders for the characters. Handled the set up of the shading networks for assets of our film in order to obtain the visual look.

RENDER WRANGLER, SENIOR PRODUCTION, UCF, ORLANDO, FLORIDA — 2011-2012
Was responsible for rendering out numerous shots. Trouble shooted issues that would arise and made sure render times were reasonable and efficient.

GRAPHIC DESIGN INTERN, THE SPOT, ORLANDO FLORIDA — 2010
Worked with a team of students to produce various work for customers. Designed business cards, tee shirts, banners, logos, letter heads, envelopes, and websites. Gained knowledge of print production work flow and had hand on training on various parts of it.

PRODUCER, ZOMBIE REHAB, ORLANDO FLORIDA — 2009
Was in charge of creating shot lists, determining locations for filming, organizing the production from pre to post. Animated the credits and worked on editing the film together.

BAKER, EINSTEIN BAGELS, ORLANDO FLORIDA — 2011
In charge of opening the store and arriving at 3 am to bake bagels and other products.

Education

University of Central Florida - 2012 - Character Animation - 3.25 GPA

Figure 2.22 Sample Résumé by Matt Justice

LAURYN DUERR

address
2961 Ashford Park Place
Oviedo, Florida 32765

tel   (321) 289-5056
email laurynduerr@yahoo.com
web   www.laurynduerr.com

specialties Texture Artist
          Editor

Skills
Proficiency in:

Maya, Premiere, Final Cut Pro, Photoshop, Microsoft Office.

Knowledge of:

Nuke, Mudbox, Illustrator.

I can learn other skills as well, very quickly and efficiently.

Experience
Editor, *UCF Visual Language Program* Orlando, FL 2011 - 2012

I worked as Editor on the short film, 'Flower Story.' Visual Language is a portfolio-restricted animation program. I, along with 25 other select people, learned all the aspects of filmmaking, while working in a team-based environment. By the end of our senior year, we created two 5 minute animated shorts to be submitted into various film festivals.

Education
University of Central Florida, Orlando, FL - Bachelor of Arts Degree in Digital Media, 2012

Dean's List, Bright Future Scholar, UCF SIGGRAPH, Digital Media Club

Brevard Community College, Titusville, FL - Associate in Arts Degree, 2008

Dean's List, Bright Futures Scholar, Band Member

Titusville High School, Titusville, FL - High School Diploma, 2007

Other Work Experience
Walt Disney World *Merchandise* Orlando, FL 2011 - Present

I work in Merchandise greeting and helping guests, checking out their purchases on a register, and making sure they have the best experience during their visit. After park hours, I help stock the stores and make sure they are ready for the upcoming day.

Barnes & Noble UCF Bookstore *Online Orders* Orlando, FL 2009 - 2010

I pulled and processed book orders, answered the phone, and took care of customers and filled their orders correctly. Working at a bookstore also means keeping boxes organized and stocking shelves.

Duerr & Cullen CPAs *Temporary Hire* Maitland, FL 2010

I was a temporary hire who helped file, type up emails for clients, and help with everything else as needed during the busy tax season.

Pumpernickel's Delicatessen *Deli Clerk* Titusville, FL 2007 - 2009

I greeted customers, took their orders and prepared their food. I also answered the phones, taking orders for the kitchen and messages for management. After hours, I cleaned the front end of the store, swept and mopped the floors, and made sure all supplies were well stocked.

Volunteer Experience
Titusville High School *Band Volunteer* Titusville, FL 2008

I helped the band director with various activities such as helping over 200 students with music and marching and also typing up documents to put into the computer.

Figure 2.23 Sample Résumé by Lauryn Duerr

WEB PRESENCE

Creating a website is an enormous undertaking. It wasn't long ago that you had to have the time and money to learn the technical aspects of coding or hire a web designer in order to get a halfway decent website. Fortunately, times have changed, and web presence no longer needs to be a fully functional website. If a fully functional website is what you desire to showcase yourself, there are now drag and drop applications available that can make the process a bit easier. There is also free website hosting available or you can simply create a blog and link to your demo reel online.

Table 2.1 lists some of the resources to help you get started.

Table 2.1 Resources to Help You Create a Website

Free Blogs	Free Website Hosting	Free Online Video
www.blogger.com	www.weebly.com	www.vimeo.com
www.wordpress.com	www.byethost.com	www.youtube.com
www.blog.com	www.yola.com	www.flickr.com
www.posterous.com	www.bix.nf	www.veoh.com

Regardless of what you decide to do, you must have presence on the web if you want people to be able to find you and see your work. Having web presence, unfortunately, also opens the doors to the possibility of someone stealing your work. The best thing to do is to watermark any images and video placed on the web. Although this won't completely prevent the possibility of theft, it does cause the thief hours of work to remove the watermark, so it is a deterrent. Thieves are everywhere. Even among the people with whom you may be currently working.

Recently, I had a friend post a link on Facebook to a website of a certain person he had worked with at a certain studio who had placed animation that he had done on her demo reel. Within 30 minutes, this girl had been mass e-mailed over 200 messages from our Facebook friends who are in the industry. Not only had she stolen his work, but also the work of two other friends of mine. I wouldn't doubt if almost everything on her demo reel was stolen. She bowed under the pressure and removed the work from her website.

The coin can also be flipped in this situation. You may be tempted to steal work and place it on your reel. Let me place this warning here. The animation industry is smaller than you think. Claiming stolen work as your own is not only illegal and immoral but will directly lead to being ostracized from the industry. Why risk everything you have worked so hard to achieve? Why would you risk losing your dreams?

Another terrific resource is www.dropbox.com. It is a free cloud space that allows you to share files easily from the public folder by creating a link to the file, which can then be e-mailed to anyone. This allows you to send files without attaching them to an e-mail directly. After creating an account, simply upload the file to the Public folder, then right mouse click over the file name from the dropbox website, copy the link to your clipboard, then paste the link into an e-mail or publish to a website.

In addition to having your portfolio on the web, you can also utilize online forums and social media websites as networking opportunities. This will be discussed in greater detail in Chapter 7.

Sample websites are shown in Figures 2.24 through 2.28 as follows:

Figure 2.24 Sample Website by Wei-Shan Yu

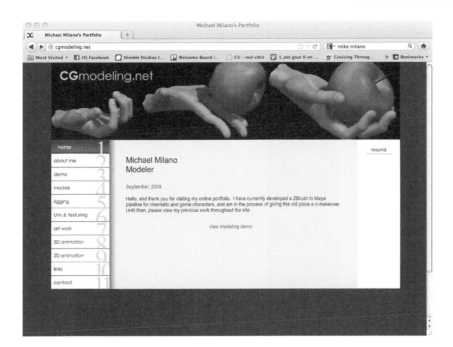

Figure 2.25 Sample Website by Michael Milano

Figure 2.26 Sample Websites

Figure 2.27 Sample Blog by Rey Ortiz

Figure 2.28 Sample Vimeo page by Randy Stratton

DEMO REEL

The demo reel is probably the most important part of your portfolio. It showcases your very best work and proves that you have the abilities to perform the job requirements if hired. Chapters 3 and 5 cover in detail what type of content you need to put in the demo reel and how to put one together. See Figure 2.29 and www.reelsuccess.com for example demo reels.

Figure 2.29 Demo Reel Title Cards by Joey Lenz, Rey Ortiz, David Bokser, and Michael Milano

THE BREAKDOWN

The breakdown accompanies your demo reel. It clarifies what you personally have done in each shot shown on your demo reel. This is where you can tell the viewer what type of software was used, how long it took you to create the shot, if you created everything or if you were part of a team, and if so, what specifically you were responsible for creating in the shot, such as animation, or modeling, or texturing. Chapter 6 covers how to create a breakdown list in detail. Sample breakdowns can be seen in Figures 2.30 and 2.31 as well as on www.reeelsuccess.com.

SUPPLEMENTARY MATERIALS

Flatbook

Some job descriptions, such as storyboard or visual development, require applicants to submit a flatbook in addition to, or in lieu of, a demo reel. A flatbook is a printed portfolio of examples of your work. The book should

Sample Breakdowns:

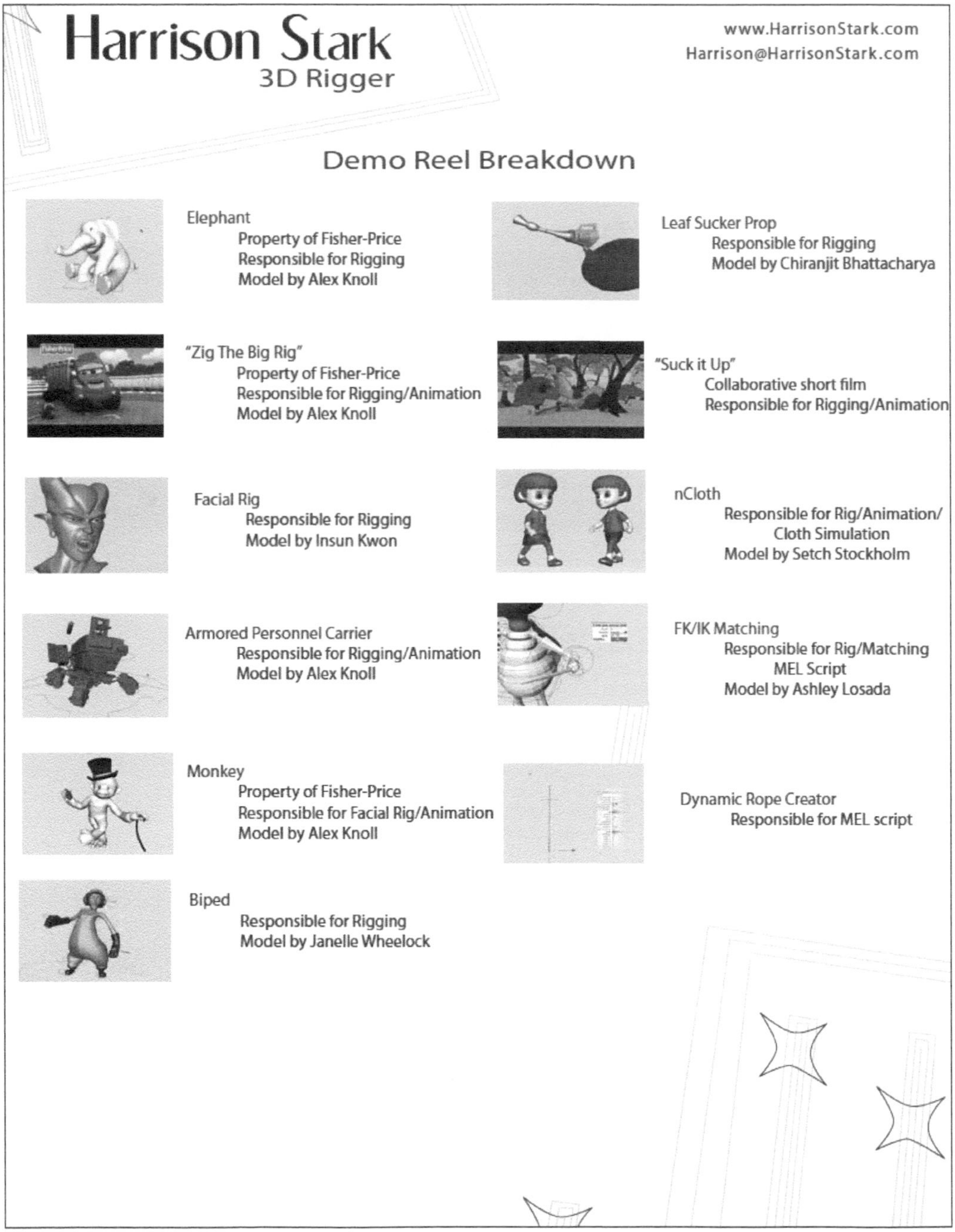

Harrison Stark
3D Rigger

www.HarrisonStark.com
Harrison@HarrisonStark.com

Demo Reel Breakdown

Elephant
 Property of Fisher-Price
 Responsible for Rigging
 Model by Alex Knoll

Leaf Sucker Prop
 Responsible for Rigging
 Model by Chiranjit Bhattacharya

"Zig The Big Rig"
 Property of Fisher-Price
 Responsible for Rigging/Animation
 Model by Alex Knoll

"Suck it Up"
 Collaborative short film
 Responsible for Rigging/Animation

Facial Rig
 Responsible for Rigging
 Model by Insun Kwon

nCloth
 Responsible for Rig/Animation/
 Cloth Simulation
 Model by Setch Stockholm

Armored Personnel Carrier
 Responsible for Rigging/Animation
 Model by Alex Knoll

FK/IK Matching
 Responsible for Rig/Matching
 MEL Script
 Model by Ashley Losada

Monkey
 Property of Fisher-Price
 Responsible for Facial Rig/Animation
 Model by Alex Knoll

Dynamic Rope Creator
 Responsible for MEL script

Biped
 Responsible for Rigging
 Model by Janelle Wheelock

Figure 2.30 *Sample Breakdown by Joey Lenz*

BREAKDOWN SHEET

Sci-fi Corridor, Software: **Maya, Photoshop, mental ray, and Nuke**

Responsibilities: **Joey Lenz - modeling, layout, procedural/file-based texturing, animation, particle fx, lighting, and compositing**
Camille Kuo - concept

The objective of this project was to gain a better understanding of moody environment lighting. With a lack of sci-fi in my current body of work, I wanted to try something different by creating a darker, dirtier piece.

Cell Phone, Software: **Maya, Photoshop, mental ray, and Nuke**

Responsibilities: **Joey Lenz - modeling, texturing, animation, lighting, and compositing**

I created an idealistic cell phone for a fake advertisement. The lighting setup for this piece was to focus on product visualization. Digital reflector boards were used to create the sharp, strong reflections seen within the surface of the cell phone model.

Telescope, Software: **Maya, Photoshop, mental ray, and Nuke**

Responsibilities: **Joey Lenz - modeling, texturing, lighting, and compositing**

This project was treated as a still-life study to challenge my artistic abilities by only using spot lights and to avoid software that renders indirect lighting effects.

Render Layers Setup Tool, Software: **Maya and text editors**

Responsibilities: **Joey Lenz - coding**

During the lighting/compositing stage, there are a lot of redundant tasks that have to manually be set up, like light linking, various render layers, and networks created in Nuke. Instead of repeating these actions, I created a few tools that automate them and shaves hours off my lighting/compositing workflow.

Hydrant, Software: **Maya, HDRShop, Photoshop, Zbrush, Mudbox, mental ray, and Nuke**

Responsibilities: **Joey Lenz - modeling, motion tracking, procedural texturing, lighting, and compositing**
Phil Liu - sculpting and texturing

To refine my live-action integration skills, I created a digital hydrant that matched the coloring and lighting of a real, motion tracked one.

Perceptions, Software: **Maya, Photoshop, mental ray, and Nuke**

Responsibilities: **Joey Lenz - vfx supervision, animation, and compositing**
Steve Lesniak - texturing, lighting, and compositing

This was one of several vfx shots I helped with for a senior film, *Perceptions*, directed by Rebekah Roediger. After a previous vfx team worked on it, we refined the shots based on the requests of the director.

Globe, Software: **Maya, Photoshop, BodyPaint, mental ray, and Nuke**

Responsibilities: **Joey Lenz - lighting and compositing**
Phil Liu - modeling and texturing

The focus of this project was projection texturing, challenging my artistic abilities by only using spot lights, and avoiding software that renders indirect lighting effects.

The Desolo Aura, Software: **Maya, Vue, Photoshop, BodyPaint, Mudbox, mental ray, and Nuke**

Responsibilities: **Joey Lenz - concept, modeling, layout, procedural texturing, rigging, animation, particle fx, lighting, and compositing**
Phil Liu - concept, finalized concept art, layout, file-based texturing, and matte painting

This was the most challenging visual effects project I have ever worked on. With just a team of two, making sure we could bring everything together, to making a cohesive design, to overcoming technical obstacles, and even faking perspective to create a grand sense of scale, was all an ambitious effort we managed to complete.

Figure 2.31 Sample Breakdown by Joey Lenz

carry out your design theme, and all pages should have a cohesive layout. Your flatbook should be printed and bound. Size format really depends on your work, but 11 × 17 inches is a nice size to have large enough images for review, but it also costs more to create a printed portfolio that size. Sample pages from a flatbook can be seen in Figure 2.32.

A terrific resource for professionally printing bound portfolios is www.lulu.com.

Figure 2.32 *Three Pages From a Sample Flatbook by Rey Ortiz*

Thank You Letter/Card or E-Mail

A well-crafted thank you letter or handwritten card can show a potential employer that you stand out in a crowd, are considerate, and pay attention to detail. You should send a thank you letter, card, or e-mail within one day following an in-person interview to anyone who was involved with your interview in any way. After the interview, make some notes about relevant points that you can use in your thank you. Take some time to reflect on what happened in the interview, and in your thank you, make sure to reinforce why your background is a perfect fit for the position. Make sure to personalize each thank you differently to each person you thank. What better way to remind those people who you are than with a specially designed thank you card that matches your portfolio theme and could even showcase an image of your artwork? Example Thank You letters can be seen in Figures 2.33 and 2.34.

An e-mail thank you is appropriate for after a phone interview. An actual letter or card would be considered overkill in this situation.

Sample Thank You Letters:

RANDY STRATTON
CHARACTER ANIMATOR

AUGUST 22, 2003

RICHARD HOLLANDER
PRESIDENT
RHYTHM AND HUES
5404 JANDY PLACE
LOS ANGELES, CA 90066

DEAR RICHARD HOLLANDER:

THANK YOU FOR TAKING THE TIME TO DISCUSS WITH ME THE POSITION OF CHARACTER
ANIMATOR. I AM EXCITED ABOUT THE POSSIBILITY OF WORKING FOR YOU AT RHYTHM AND
HUES, AND I KNOW MY BACKGROUND AS A COMPUTER ART MAJOR HAS PREPARED ME TO
CREATE ANIMATION EFFECTIVELY.

YOU MENTIONED DURING OUR CONVERSATION THAT YOU WERE EAGER TO FILL THIS POSITION
AS SOON AS POSSIBLE. I BELIEVE I CAN MEET THAT NEED AS I GRADUATED FROM THE
SAVANNAH COLLEGE OF ART AND DESIGN ON MAY 31 AND AM AVAILABLE TO WORK ANY
TIME THEREAFTER.

I LOOK FORWARD TO HEARING FROM YOU SOON, AND IF YOU HAVE ANY ADDITIONAL
QUESTIONS ABOUT MY BACKGROUND OR QUALIFICATIONS, PLEASE DO NOT HESITATE TO
CALL. I CAN BE REACHED AT (912) 355 2170.

SINCERELY,

RANDY STRATTON

1139 MARIBOB CIRCLE
SAVANNAH, GEORGIA 31406

MORPHEOUS_S@YAHOO.COM

Figure 2.33 Sample Thank You Letter by Randy Stratton

Mr.

Address

Dear _____:

Thank you so much for taking time from your busy schedule to meet with me last week. It was very helpful to me to learn so much about the current projects of _____ and the career paths of several of your staff. I appreciate your reviewing my portfolio and encouraging my career plans.

Based on what I learned from talking to you and other research I have done, I am very interested in being considered for employment with your studio in the future. I will be available to begin work after I graduate in May 2008. As you saw from my portfolio, I have developed strong skills in the area of texture and concept art and this is a good match for the types of projects in which your studio specializes. I have enclosed a copy of my resume to serve as a reminder of my background, some of which I discussed with you when we met.

During the next few months I will stay in contact with you in hopes that there may be an opportunity to join your team. Thank you again for your generous help.

Sincerely,

Rey Ortiz

3408 Montgomery St.
Apt. A   reycomvisuals@yahoo.com
Savannah, GA 31405

REYOrtiz
concept & texture artist

Figure 2.34 *Sample Thank You Letter by Rey Ortiz*

RECOMMENDED READING LIST

Design Workshop by Robin Williams

Letterhead and Logo Design 12 by Oxide Design Co.

Letterhead and Logo Design 11 by Design Army

Simple Web Sites: Organizing Content-Rich Web Sites Into Simple Structures by Stefan Mumaw

What Color Is Your Parachute? 2013 by Richard N. Bolles

BASIC DESIGN RULES

DO's AND DON'Ts

- Don't market yourself as a company, unless you are starting your own company.
- Be creative. If you are applying for a creative position, show your creativity. After all, you are not applying to be in bank management.
- Have someone with a good grasp of the language to proofread your e-mail, cover letter, résumé, and other printed materials.
- Tailor all materials to each job application.
- Be sure to consider your identity in your name, or possible name changes, before marketing yourself.
- Don't be tempted to design odd-shaped or -sized business cards.
- Print homemade business cards only on a laser printer.
- Don't use perforated business card sheets.
- Create space for writing notes on the front or back of your business card.
- Don't imbed images or documents into an e-mail.
- Use links to your website, downloadable, or streamable materials inside e-mails.
- Address your cover letter to an actual person.
- Don't tell a potential employer what you want.
- Tell a potential employer what you bring to the table.
- Have web presence.
- Use watermarks to protect your work online.
- Be clear about the work you have done.

- Don't put work that you didn't create into your portfolio.
- Spend most of your time creating or polishing your portfolio pieces, not on creating the portfolio design.

ACTION LIST

BRAINSTORMING

- Research business card and letterhead design ideas.
- Gather dates and information for résumé content.
- Research business card printing companies.
- Decide whether you will have a full portfolio website, post only your reel, or have a blog.
- Gather images for flatbook and/or website.

CREATING

- Thumbnail 10–20 different layout ideas for your business card and letterhead.
- From the thumbnails, narrow the ideas down to 2 or 3.
- Design your business card with a bleed. Don't forget to consider the safe zone as well.
- Design letterhead for both digital and print media. Make sure to design your letterhead in conjunction with your business card.
- Have your business cards printed.
- Create your résumé.
- Write a sample cover letter for practice and to have as a beginning template for when you are ready to actually write one.
- Register your URL or obtain a blog.
- Design online presence.
- Create your Flatbook if you have decided to have one. Use the same basic design that you have developed for your business card and letterhead for your page layout so that you have a unified portfolio package.
- Design a Thank You card that matches your overall cohesive design, or purchase some premade cards to have on hand.
- Write a sample Thank You letter to have as a beginning template for when you are ready to actually write one.

CHAPTER 3

GATHERING CONTENT: WHAT DO YOU PUT INTO THE REEL?

Student: Um, can you show me like, the lowest common denominator reel? The lowest quality of work you can show and still get a job?

My Response: This is the level of work that you are competing with. If you don't feel ready to compete, then you should continue to work on improving yourself.

GATHERING CONTENT—WHAT TO PUT INTO THE REEL

Every demo reel that you send out should be created and tailored specifically to the job description for the position to which you are applying. Apply for only the positions that you want or that could possibly lead into a position that you want, and do not include anything else on your reel. Don't put anything on your reel unless you want to be hired and working in that position. If you are an animator, don't show off your modeling talent on your animation reel. Stay with the specific discipline for which you are applying. A great example of a entry level character animator demo reel can be seen in Figure 3.1 and on www.reelsuccess.com.

Something I hear from people all the time is that they are not really sure what they want to do. Usually they like three or more areas of specialization or just love everything to do with the animation production pipeline. Although this is not necessarily a bad thing, to a potential employer, it looks as if you actually don't know what you want to do and expect the employer to find a place to fit you into their pipeline. Most applicants think this is a good thing, because it makes you more flexible, but employers don't want to have to spend so much time analyzing your portfolio to figure out where you would fit best. For this reason, the clearer you are about what you want to do, the easier it will be to land an interview and a potential job.

Figure 3.1 Stills From a Remarkable Character Animator Demo Reel by Becki Tower. This demo reel enabled her to get an internship at Neversoft to work on Guitar Hero III. *Before completeing her internship, she also received an apprenticeship at Blue Sky Studios to work on* Horton Hears a Who. *Updating her reel with her work from her Blue Sky apprenticeship, she landed an animation apprenticeship with Pixar Studios*

Try to figure out where your strengths lie. Ask teachers, friends, parents, or post your work online and ask for feedback. Backwards engineering your ideal job is the perfect way of figuring out what you really want to do and how exactly to get there. Sometimes it can be as easy as choosing a specific studio that would be your dream place to work. Knowing where you want to work is very helpful when figuring out what you should show on your demo reel. The work you show to Pixar, a full feature animation studio, is very different from the work you would show to Industrial, Light, and Magic, a studio which works with integrating animation into live-action. The same goes for gaming companies. Two companies, such as Valve and Disney Interactive, can be very different in their styles. Make sure your work reflects the companies that most interest you.

Once you have decided where you want to be, you can figure out how to get there. I always compare this process to traveling. When a person travels, they usually have a destination in mind. From that destination decision, a specific route can be determined. Some take the fastest path, whereas others prefer the scenic route. Both will eventually lead the traveller to the destination, but the scenic route is typically more interesting and usually takes longer to get there. There are also travellers

It is better to travel well than to arrive.

Buddha

who don't have a specific destination in mind. They simply embark on a journey and delight in the places they come across, no matter where they go.

A career in animation can be very similar to traveling. You must first decide what kind of person you are. Do you prefer the fastest, most direct path, or are you an adventurer? I think Figure 3.2 is a great visualization of this. It is a photo I took while hiking to Heceta Head Lighthouse on the Oregon Coast. If I had just kept on going, I would have never seen this beautiful image if I had not stopped and turned around to search for the sound of a babbling creek that I had heard.

> Once you make a decision, the universe conspires to make it happen.
>
> Ralph Waldo Emerson

Figure 3.2 Do You Prefer the Fastest, Most Direct Path, or Are You an Adventurer?

Dedicate an external hard drive specifically for your demo reel and portfolio. This would allow you to specify storage space and organize all of your work in one place. As you gather your work together, create a folder structure like the one in the example below in Figure 3.3, that organizes your files and makes them easily accessible.

Figure 3.3 Example Folder Structure for Demo Reel and Portfolio Files

SPECIALIZATION REELS VERSUS GENERALIZATION REELS

A smaller company or boutique shop is going to be looking for more generalized talent, because they cannot afford to hire as many people to fill specialized areas. The larger the company, the more specialized you will need to be. A specialized reel should show work in only one area. If you have work that fits into other areas, put those on your website, or edit together a general reel in addition to your specialized reel. You could even have several different types of reels based on the amount of work you have, such as an animation reel, a rigging reel, and a general reel as in Figure 3.4.

> A real decision is measured by the fact that you've taken a new action. If there's no action, you haven't truly decided.
>
> Tony Robbins

Figure 3.4 Opening Titles of Two Amazing Reels From the Same Talented Guy, David Bokser

Just because you are specialized, however, does not mean you should not have experience with all aspects of the production pipeline and process. The more you know, the more hirable you are and the more likely you are to keep a full-time position if you have the ability to transfer to a different department when the project you are working on moves on through the pipeline and your specific job is finished on a project. Your ideal goal would be to become a specialized generalist, who understands and can work in all aspects of the production pipeline, with at least one area of specialization.

WHAT TO INCLUDE OR NOT TO INCLUDE?

ORIGINAL BEST WORK

Putting together a demo reel is really much simpler than most people make it out to be. Only put your best original work on your reel. That's it. Very simple.

The problem is that most people, especially when starting out, want to put everything they have ever done on their reel. Every project becomes like a child, and you become like an annoying stage mother. They are so proud of what they have created that they are blind to see that it's really not that good.

Or they are the exact opposite. They become overly critical. They think that everything they have done isn't good enough, so they never get around to putting a reel together and continue working at their local retail job making minimum wage.

The ideal situation here is to put on a critical eye, review what work you do have, and choose the best three pieces to put on your reel.

Showing that you can use industry standard software is a must. Most of the larger studios use proprietary software, which means it is software that has been developed in-house. However, some of them do use off the shelf software as part of their production pipeline. Be sure that you keep up with what is being used in the industry. For example, Shake was the industry-standard software for compositing not too long ago. Now it is Nuke. Tomorrow it may be something different. The most important thing however is that you can demonstrate proficiency in the area in which you are applying.

There are two reasons to go to graduate school: 1. To hone your skills and 2. To one day teach. Graduate school is an opportunity to work collaboratively and also work around people who will push you to push yourself. Quite frankly, some people work better with deadlines.

Many of the software companies provide student or educational versions for a discounted price compared to professional licenses. However, in order to get the student pricing, you must be registered as a full-time student or teach at one of the acceptable schools. Is very important to note that if you are using an academic license, you are not allowed to use that software at a freelance or contract position.

ONGOING PORTFOLIO DEVELOPMENT

Once you have put together your reel and begin to look for work, continue to work on new projects. Challenge yourself to complete one new project every week or two. By doing this you will continue to enhance your skills and always have new work to place on your reel. Practice makes perfect. There is a catch to that phrase. The more you practice, the better you will get ONLY if you are deliberate when you practice. Push yourself to excel. Watch online tutorials regularly. Challenge yourself with projects that will enhance and strengthen your abilities. Only then will practice pay off. Think about athletes. The ones that succeed are the ones that push themselves and their bodies during their daily practice.

While you are working on new projects, you may find that some of them, while not finished, are actually better than one of the pieces on your reel. You can actually put Work-in-Progress (WIP) on your reel. Just make sure you label it as WIP. Otherwise, your website or blog is a great place to show off what you are currently working on. By methodically posting your work to forums for feedback or your blog to keep a record, you are also documenting your progress. This is great for potential employers to view when they are trying to analyze your work methods. It is also a great idea to keep track of the time you spend working. One interview question that always arises is, "How long did it take you to complete this piece."

I know you've heard it a thousand times before. But it's true—hard work pays off. If you want to be good, you have to practice, practice, practice. If you don't love something, then don't do it.

Ray Bradbury

LOW-RESOLUTION PREVIEWS OR RENDERS

Low-resolution previews of your work are acceptable, like a playblast in Maya or Flipbook in Houdini, depending on your specialization. Obviously, if you are applying for a lighting position, you will have to fully render your work. But animators and modelers can use previews acceptably on their reels if you are in a pinch for time and don't have the luxury of lighting and rendering your work. Remember that your time spent should be on what you are creating and your area of focus. So if you want to be an animator, spend your time animating, not lighting and rendering. Once the animation piece is finished, move on and work on a new animation.

STILL IMAGES

Do not add still images to your demo reel. Save those for your website. You can include still images if they're part of a progression to show your work process, but don't just display a slideshow to music. This goes for drawings as well as still frame renders. If you are an environment artist and you want to show off your environment, have the camera shift subtly to show off the dimensions of your environment. Slow, controlled camera movements are the best. You don't want the camera flying through the environment abruptly and making your viewer nauseous. You can also have elements of the environment animated, such as trees blowing in the wind or birds flying across the sky, to give some life and interest to your scene.

HOW LONG?

Your demo reel should be no longer than 3–4 minutes. That is if you have been working in the industry for some time, many years. For a student or someone new entering the industry, 30 seconds of really wonderful and GREAT work is adequate. Thirty seconds of your best work is much better than 3–4 minutes of fluff. It's good to put together a short reel and a long reel, but most students end up with only a short reel. This is just fine. Twenty to thirty seconds of highly polished, wonderful work will get you an interview, and they will want to see what else you can do. It will pique their interest and make them take notice. Just make sure you have additional finished pieces or WIPs for them to see once you get to the interview.

HOW MUCH TO INCLUDE?

Show a variety of works and styles. However, do not spend your time doing so many different things that everything you include is mediocre. Take the time to really polish 3–5 of your pieces and present those. We're talking quality not quantity. Just keep repeating that: quality, not quantity. Make your demo reel represent the very best that you can do. Remember the demo reel is how you're going to get an interview. You will be judged by the worst piece on your demo reel, not your best. The reason for this is because whomever is looking at your reel will then question your judgment of what is aesthetically good. They assume you are showing your very best work. So, if it is not your best, leave it off.

LEGALITIES

For demo reel purposes, anything shown on your reel should be your original creation and, if not, should be noted in the breakdown. The breakdown is covered in detail in Chapter 6.

Any work that you do professionally belongs to the studio or person for whom you are working. Always clarify when accepting a job whether you can use the work that you do on your demo reel. Some companies do not allow work to ever be used on a demo reel. Other studios have certain time periods, like once a film goes to DVD or BluRay, or once the game title has been on the market for 6 months. Talk with both the Human Resources department and your immediate supervisors to find out what the policy is for that particular company. You really don't want to burn any bridges in this industry.

One question I get often is if it is legal to use copyrighted music on your reel. The answer to this is yes, it is fine, as long as you aren't publishing your reel on YouTube. However, let me just say that EVERYONE I have ever spoke to about music on demo reels has said the same thing, "don't bother with music, we don't listen to it anyway." Chapter 5 covers more information about using music on your reel.

CONTENT RECOMMENDATIONS

Remember, regardless of your area of specialization, companies prefer to see work that looks similar to what they already actually create. If your creative work doesn't look at all like anything they do, then they can't visualize you as part of their team. So, make sure you do your research and apply to companies that are aligned with your creative style, talents, and abilities. Demo reels are your visual resume that proves you have the abilities to do whatever the job description lists as required qualifications.

The reel should show your best work and, when possible, the process you used to achieve your end result. Showing your process is almost as important as showing your abilities. This process allows others to partially get inside of your head and see how you work.

The best thing to do is to take a look at several job postings that are related to your career interests. Begin making a list of the required qualifications and compare these to the kind of work you already have. From there, you can identify what you can use on a reel and what else you need to create. It is best to spend some time developing work to fill out the gaps you are missing while you are searching and applying for job openings. You will also notice that there is quite a bit of overlap between specializations. This is one reason why it is best to become a generalist with a specialized focus. What follows is a description of the most common specialization jobs and suggestions of what to include in your portfolio or reel.

CONCEPT ARTIST

A concept artist is between the director and the production team and is responsible for all the initial artwork that is developed for the look and style of characters, sets, props, color scripts, and other art. As a concept artist, you should show as many of your concepts as possible. Organize them into categories of style or separate them by characters and environments.

Just don't put a slideshow together and call it your demo reel. Most concept artists begin their careers as a storyboard artist.

One of the best still image demo reels that I've seen was a concept art reel by one of my students as seen in Figure 3.5. He did a wonderful job showing his concept drawings and how they built up to the final image that was created in 3D. He even added animations of his concepts once they were completed.

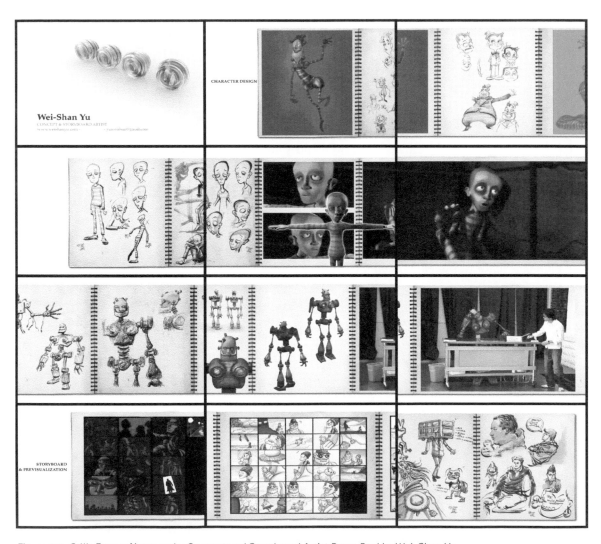

Figure 3.5 Stills From a Noteworthy Concept and Storyboard Artist Demo Reel by Wei-Shan Yu

STORYBOARD ARTIST

The Storyboard Artist translates and interprets written story into a visual story by creating sketches, thumbnail drawings and finished storyboard drawings. The storyboard demo reel is usually a 2D animatic, or sections of multiple animatics. In this animatic, you need to show your storytelling techniques utilizing film language with effective use of camera, staging, and pacing. Your ideas should be creative and show the development of character personality.

Storyboard artists must be able to quickly sketch thumbnails, so showing initial sketches is just as important as the fully finished and detailed storyboard panels on your demo reel. The reel should show evidence of a strong ability to draw characters and action.

LAYOUT ARTIST (ANIMATION PRODUCTION) AND PREVISUALIZATION ARTIST (LIVE-ACTION PRODUCTION)

Layout Artists take completed 2D storyboards and compose the 3D shots by positioning and animating the camera. They usually, while working closely with the director and editor, determine the initial length of each shot. They are first in the pipeline to build locations, including major props, block in the position of characters, select camera angles, and plot camera moves.

A Previsualization Artist's job is similar to a Layout Artists. Previsualization (previs) uses simplified 3D graphics to plan live-action or visual effects sequences and camera moves before they are filmed. A Previsualization Artist works closely with the director to make live-action filming more efficient by working out camera angles and complex staging.

A layout/previs reel should exhibit your best camera work, blocking, and composition. Show a sequence of shots (as opposed to random shots) cut together that were created for an edit. Your camera work should show a strong understanding of camera language and cinematic storytelling such as framing, perspective, coverage, continuity, and camera movement. Evidence that the Layout/Previs Artist is a 3D generalist is also a good idea.

MODELER: AKA CHARACTER ARTIST OR ENVIRONMENT ARTIST

Modelers are responsible for creating the 3D computer assets for a production. A good modeler can create both clean low-resolution models and highly detailed models using normal maps and sculpting tools.

Modelers should also have excellent UV layout skills and be able to show a mastery of texture creation tools (normal, diffuse, specularity, ambient occlusion, etc.) using software such as Zbrush, ddo/ndo, and Xnormal. Smaller studios or productions may also require modelers to rig, texture, and light their models.

There are two areas of concentration in modeling that larger studios tend to look for when hiring a modeler:

1. Organic modelers. Figure 3.6 are stills from an organic modeling demo reel. An organic modeling demo reel should show work that involves different types of characters: biped, human, creatures, animals, insects, and wings. Evidence that you understand edge loops and deformation is essential. Models should be rigged and moving to show deformations. If you aren't good at rigging, team up with a rigger and you both will benefit. Organic modelers are also referred to as character artists.

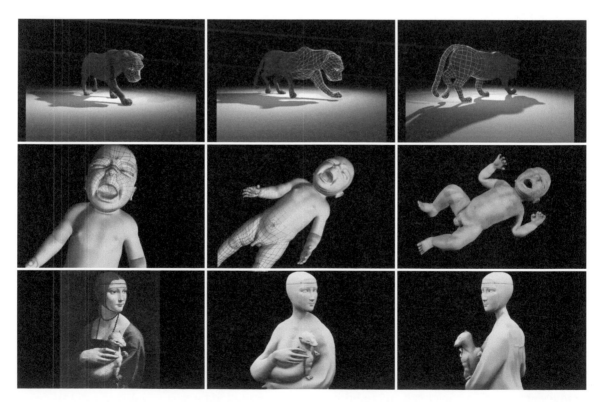

Figure 3.6 Stills From a Wonderful Character Artist Reel From the Gifted Michael Milano. You can see his student work at cgmodeling.net and compare how much he has grown as an artist since then on his professional site, cgmodeling.com

2. Hard surface modelers. A hard surface modeling demo reel should show work that involves different types of buildings, vehicles, and props. Hard surface modelers are also referred to as Environment Artists.

Regardless of your concentration, modelers must show an ability to create accurate models using design reference. This is where showing your process is essential. Show a turntable of your model with the wireframe with the reference images as well. Your style should match the style of the larger studio to which you are applying. Smaller studios want to see a range of styles in your work.

CHARACTER RIGGER

A Character Rigger designs and creates the skeletal structure and control system for CG models that need to be animated, which can include humans, creatures, and objects. Character Riggers are also responsible for skinning and deformation weighting (enveloping), creating facial shapes, creating and supporting interfaces, and developing tools and pipeline solutions to support the animation team. In addition, the Character Rigger may also be expected to add secondary motions and deformations to a character using muscles, dynamics, fur, hair, or cloth.

A Character Rigger should have working knowledge of scripting languages, such as MEL and Python; a thorough knowledge of character kinematics, deformation, and biomechanics; basic skills in modeling and an understanding of mesh flow. Character Riggers should have an eye for detail and a passion for problem solving.

A rigging demo reel see Figure 3.7 and on www.reelsuccess.com should show demonstrations of a variety of different types of rigging solutions for different types of characters: bipeds, quadrupeds, creatures, wings, tails, insects, facial, props, skinning deformation solutions. Demonstrations of scripting tools, interfaces, and secondary motion systems should also be shown. When applying to a game company, a rigging reel should show an understanding of the limitations of the game engine.

CHARACTER ANIMATOR

A Character Animator brings characters to life. In addition to technical ability, artistic skill, and a creative mind, a Character Animator must have a feel for movement and timing, honed observational skills, acting talent, and be able to take direction.

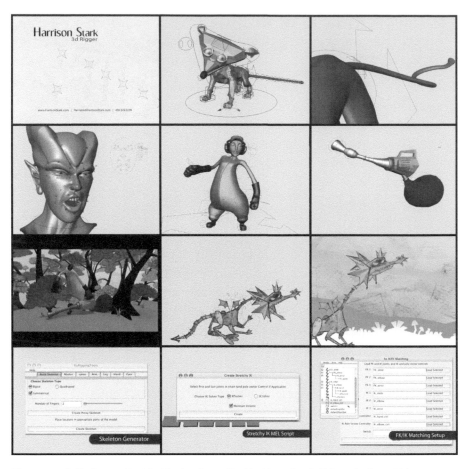

Figure 3.7 Stills From a Terrific Rigging Demo Reel by Harry Stark. This reel allowed him to obtain an internship at Fisher Price. Harry was a technical animator as part of the Visual Effects team on Life of PI, which won the Academy Award in 2013 for best Visual Effects.

A character animation demo reel should contain examples of the following: LipSync, two characters interacting with each other, acting, one- and two-handed object interactions, lifting a heavy object, subtlety and emotion, emotional reaction, an impact (being hit by an object), action, backflips, and choreographed movement (dancing or fighting). Additional animation using props, quadrupeds, and/or any other creature other than a biped will set your demo reel apart from the rest. When applying to a game company, an animation reel should show also show cycles: running, walking, dying, holding and reloading a weapon, falling, and jumping. It is even better to show these cycles functioning inside a game engine like Unity, which you can download for free from Unity3d.com.

Don't be afraid to share your thought process on your demo reel: show your thumbnails, your reference videos, and your final animation. If you don't want to include all of this on your reel, you can have it available on your website.

LOOK DEVELOPMENT/SURFACING ARTIST

A Look Developer/Surfacing Artist is responsible for creating and maintaining the desired surface look and feel for characters, props, and environments. Part of this process is not only creating textures (using photography of existing texture and 2D or 3D painting software like Mari, Mudbox, or Zbrush) but also working with the texture team when creating complex material networks. They work closely with the lighting team and shader writers.

The demo reel should consist of models and environments with various styles and surfaces.

LIGHTING ARTIST

Lighting Artists do so much more than add light to a scene. With an eye for esthetics and strong technical skills, a Lighting Artist creates atmosphere and shapes what the final look of the scene will be. They are responsible for creating beautiful and convincing images that are efficient to render. They should also have a general understanding of compositing and surfacing.

A good lighting demo reel shows proper understanding for depth, tone, form, color, shadows, and composition. The reel should contain examples that demonstrate a solid knowledge of how the placement and intensity of lights can be used to set a mood and direct the eye through the use of various types of contrast, such as value, color, and depth of field, within both a stylized and highly photo-realistic style. Demonstration of an understanding of how light interacts with different materials, textures, particles, and fluids are also necessary.

A demo reel being used to obtain work in live-action should also show an applicable knowledge of HDRI and the ability to match lighting and shadows.

EFFECTS ARTIST

An Effects Artist creates digital simulations that are based on physics models and procedural mathematical algorithms. Effects Artists work using simulations, such as particle simulations to create dust, fire, smoke, haze, rain, snow, fur, hair, and cloth simulations, as well as crowd simulations that populate a scene with many people. Because Effects Artists work toward the end of the pipeline, they are sometimes called upon to model, animate, light, rig, or basically do anything necessary to get the shot finished. As one friend told me, by the time a shot gets to the FX department, everyone else who worked on the shot preceding them has been reassigned to another project, so if anything needs to be corrected, it is up to him as the FX artist to fix it.

An effects demo reel should show a variety of believable simulations, such as dust, fire, smoke, haze, rain, snow, fur, hair, cloth, and crowds. Show your thought process, and don't be afraid to show reference.

COMPOSITOR

A Compositor takes images from multiple sources, either live-action or CG, and brings all the elements together to create a final seamless image that matches the desired look or feel for the production, and if done successfully, looks as if the film was captured on set by a single camera by the use of color correction, keying, and the various other tools available. There are junior positions that also fall under the job description of a compositor, which, in larger companies, can be held by entry-level professionals: Matte Painter, Roto/Paint/Prep Artist, and Matchmove/ Camera Tracker.

Matte Painter

A Matte Painter creates background paintings that are usually used by the compositors but may also be used by the Environment Artist and rendered in multiple layers. The background paintings can be anything from 2D images to 3D digital set extension models for live-action plates, or even an entirely modeled city full of CG elements that are lit to match the live-action plate.

Roto/Paint/Prep Artist

A Roto/Paint/Prep Artist works in live-action and does the systematic and painstaking job of isolating a specific object from a photographic plate, often frame by frame. One of my friends' first jobs was to paint Mystique's eyes yellow in the X-Men (2000) frame by frame. The Roto Artist is responsible for digitally cutting out a foreground actor frame by frame, if necessary, if they were not filmed on a green or blue screen. The Roto Artist may also be called upon to do tracking marker removals, and other clean-up work for live-action plates.

Matchmoving/Camera Tracking Artist

Matchmoving/Camera Tracking Artist tracks the live-action camera movement in 3D and creates a 3D camera that will allow the CG artists to match the placement and motion of the CG elements to the live-action background plate. The Matchmover is also responsible for tracking moving characters, environments, props, or vehicles from the live-action plate whenever a 3D object or character interacts with the live-action plate.

A Compositing demo reel should show image breakdowns by showing the original plate and each subsequent stage added to achieve the final resulting image, such as color correction and keying. Examples should include successful rotoscoping, matchmoving, camera tracking, color correction, green screen keying, animating garbage mattes for cleanup, as well as integration of set extensions and matte paintings.

3D DEPTH/STEREOSCOPIC CONVERSION ARTIST

The 3D Depth Artist works in a company focused on stereoscopic conversion and must creatively interpret and apply stereo concepts. The 3D Depth Artist must have a good "stereo eye," a strong understanding of 3D space, and an applicable knowledge of Compositing as a foundation.

The 3D Depth Artist shows examples of converted shots on a 2D reel by rendering into anaglyph or by showing the depth layer in the image breakdown.

TECHNICAL ARTIST

The Technical Artist is someone who balances and excels in both technical and artistic skills. The Technical Artist thrives in an environment where creative problem solving is needed. Usually a go-between, the Technical Artist understands and can communicate the needs and desires of the artists to the programmers and vice versa. The job description of a Technical Artist differs from company to company, but usually includes someone who is a talented artist (knows how to draw, rig, animate, etc.) and who is also proficient in at least one programming language and scripting (C++, Python, MEL, etc.). The Technical Artist is usually responsible for creating tools using programming and scripting to help improve the efficiency of their production team.

The Technical Artist is not an entry-level position. In animation production, Technical Artists are referred to as technical directors, or TDs, and are generally specialized to a particular area. The best way to become a TD is to begin in one of the specialty areas such as modeling, lighting, rigging, character, or effects.

MOTION GRAPHICS DESIGNER

Motion Graphics Designers are individuals who create content for film, television, online, and mobile devices featuring animation and visual effects. Motion Graphics Designers are a unique amalgam of graphic designer, filmmaker, and animator. The content they create include, but is not limited to commercials, film title sequences, television series opening sequences, animated branding, digital signage, and network identity.

The motion graphics demo reel should show clips of example work of created content and is probably the exception when it comes to using music on a reel. Motions Graphics Designers need to show that their work is creatively current. The reel must show the range of creative and technical abilities.

ACTION LIST

BRAINSTORMING

- Identify your specialization area.
- Identify the type of studio or style your work reflects, live-action visual effects, feature animation, game art, or motion graphics.
- Gather content already created and organize onto a hard drive.
- Make a list of content that needs further work or refinement.
- Make a list of content that needs to be rendered.
- Begin looking for music if you are inclined to use some. Remember, no one listens while watching your reel.
- Make a list of content that is missing from your specialization area so that you can create future projects that fill the void.

CREATING

- Rework any content that needs to be polished.
- Re-render or create low-resolution files (like playblasts in Maya) of any work necessary. You may need to render out separate passes of plates if you are showing an image breakdown progression of your work.
- Begin work on any content that needs to be created specifically for your demo reel. Consider incorporating your name and contact information as one of these projects.

CHAPTER 4

TARGETING SPECIFIC STUDIOS— WHAT DO STUDIOS WANT TO SEE?

Advice is like snow—the softer it falls, the longer it dwells upon, and
the deeper in sinks into the mind.

—Samuel Taylor Coleridge

Finding a job is a mixture of being prepared and being in the right place at
the right time. For this reason, once you have a great portfolio of work, move
to the location where you want to work. Studios often hire people simply
based on availability, especially if they want to finish up a project and need
extra help. This will get your foot in the door and possibly hired on for future
projects.

Here are some ideas of how to relocate that I have experienced or have been
told about by others:

1. Find work locally at a national retail or restaurant chain then transfer
   to the new area. This will provide you with a day job while you are
   searching for your first position in the animation industry. This plan,
   however, could take months to years, depending on the employer and
   definitely do not mention this until you are ready to transfer.
2. Save enough money to live 3–6 months while you beat the pavement
   looking for work.
3. Couch surf: www.couchsurfing.org is a website that connects people
   who need a place to stay with others willing to provide a couch for a
   night or two.
4. Hosteling: www.hostels.com This could be an option in certain places,
   and if you can afford a bed for a while. If an opening comes available
   from someone else leaving, many of them will let you work a few hours
   a day in exchange for a bed.

If moving to that location is not feasible, there are other options. I have known some people who acquired a cell phone with a local phone number and also a physical mailing address from the UPS store so that the studios thought they lived in the area. If you do this just make sure you have enough cash available to get on a plane immediately if someone should call for an interview. It is time to think outside of the box.

TARGETING SPECIFIC STUDIOS—WHAT DO STUDIOS WANT TO SEE?

Your work should match the quality and style of the studio that you're applying to. For example, the work that is done at a feature animation studio like Pixar or DreamWorks is very different from that of a visual effects studio like Digital Domain or Industrial Light and Magic. If Rhythm & Hues is one of the places you want to work, then you better make sure that you have some animals that are animated, then integrated and interacting with live action on your demo reel. Research the company that you're applying to and see what it is they do. Make sure that your work would fit in there. If it doesn't, and you really want to work there, then you need to create some work specifically for that studio. If you don't have work that meets the job description, don't send in a reel for that job. The studio will appreciate you not wasting their time.

To get the latest input from industry professionals, I sent out an anonymous survey in December 2012. Responses came in from people, who are freelancers, contract animators, or have worked at a variety of large and small studios including:

Activision Blizzard

Bigpoint, Inc

Blind Squirrel Digital

Blue Sky Studios

Blur Studios

Daktronics Creative Services

Digital Domain

Disney Animation

Dreamworks Animation, SKG

Electronic Arts

Framestore

Hi-Rez Studios

Hooah LLC.

Human Head Studios, Inc.

Humoring the Fates Animation Studio

Industrial Light & Magic

Lucid SFX Development

Microsoft

The Mission Studio

Method Studios

NBC—Network

Neversoft Entertainment

Newbreed VFX

Ninjaneer Studios

Playdom

RGH Entertainment

Reel FX

Rockstar Games

Runic Games

Sony Pictures Animation

Sony Pictures Imageworks

ILM

Walsh Family Media, New York

Walt Disney Feature Animation

Weta Digital

Approximately 84% of the respondents stated that the studios where they work do hire for positions at the entry level, 49% of those studios offer internships, and approximately 14% offer apprenticeships as seen in Figure 4.1.

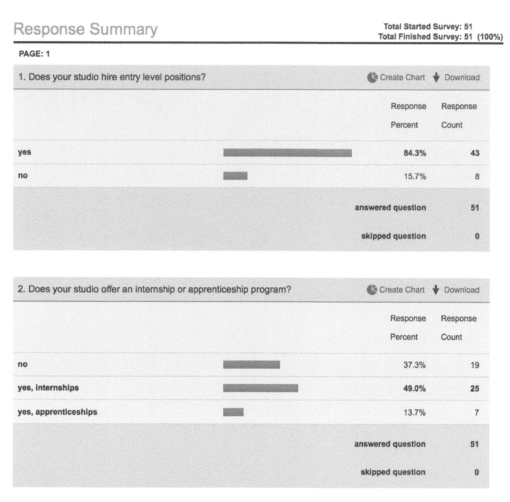

Figure 4.1 Bar Graph Showing the Results of an Anonymous Survey

HOW TO FIND ENTRY-LEVEL STUDIO JOBS

Studios use various resources to advertise job positions. Approximately 33% of the studios they work for use the professional networking site, LinkedIn. com. Only 6% use Animation World Network's job board (awn.com) and Creative Heads.net, as seen in Figure 4.2.

3. What resources does your studio use to advertise job postings?		Create Chart ⬇ Download	
		Response Percent	Response Count
linkedin.com		33.3%	17
creativeheads.net		5.9%	3
awn.com		5.9%	3
word of mouth		54.9%	28
		Other (please specify) Show Responses	37
		answered question	51
		skipped question	0

Figure 4.2 Bar Graph Showing the Results of an Anonymous Survey

Most studios do have job or career sections on their own website. www .cgstudiomap.com is a great resource that pinpoints the location of many of the studios located worldwide. By clicking on the studio, you get all their contact information and a link to their website.

In addition to the main company website, such as disneycareers.com or www .rhythm.com/jobs, other online sites used by the studios to advertise job postings include the following:

awn.com

animationguild.org

CGHub.org

creativeplanetnetwork.com

creativeheads.net (SIGGRAPH.org)

gamasutra.com

gameguzzler.com

internships.com

Polycount.com

Some of the major studios have a university relations program. Check with your alma mater alumni office or career services to see if they are connected to any of those programs. Also check with them to see if the school is registered with any resource such as collegecentral.com, to help their alumni get jobs.

ADDITIONAL TIPS BY RESPONDENTS OF THE SURVEY

- Studios also contact people (who have previously applied) as a follow-up when they are hiring to see if they want to update their materials in order to be considered.
- Company websites generally list the most accurate up-to-date job openings. This seems to be the case in most small studios in the video game industry. Creativeheads.net is somewhat useful as well, although studios that advertise through those websites tend to be larger. This generally means you are dealing with Human Resources (HR) first, and it can be a bit more difficult to get through to a creative director or animation director.
- Since so much of the work is contract based, managers often call artists with a proven track record that they have worked with in the past.
- Start-up companies and smaller studios have historically been more open to hiring entry-level or junior artists.
- There are certain major studios that do hire entry-level positions. Most of these studios have developed internship or apprenticeship programs that are offered every year. Some require current enrollment in a college or university course or program.

NETWORKING—IT'S NOT JUST WHAT YOU KNOW, BUT WHOM YOU KNOW

> It's all about people. It's about networking and being nice to people and not burning any bridges.
>
> Mike Davidson

Of the respondents surveyed, approximately 55% of the studios they work for used word-of-mouth to advertise open job positions. This means basically that they ask their current employees whether they know any talented digital artists, animators, and so on who could fill the position. It's not only about what you know but also about whom you know. Every person you meet is a potential connection. Be sure to always treat everyone you meet with respect because you never know whom you might be talking to. One friend of mine was dropping off some requested information after hours and had a conversation in the elevator with whom he thought was the building janitor. The next day, his contact at the studio mentioned to him that he had heard that my friend had met the studio owner in the elevator the evening before and that the owner's first impression of him was very good.

SOCIAL NETWORKING SITES

LinkedIn, Facebook, and Twitter seem to be social networking sites that are utilized the most by the animation and gaming industries. Not only do they use these sites as tools for marketing and promotion, they also use them for recruiting new employees. If you don't currently use these sites, you should really consider creating accounts on all three sites for networking opportunities. You can "follow" or "like" whatever studios interest you as potential employers. Some of these studios have specific groups or accounts setup for recruiting purposes and send out postings when there are job openings. Others provide tips and can be a great resource for initial networking. Just be extremely cautious with your profile. Remember, anything you write down may at some point become public. Do not write anything or publish photos anywhere that you wouldn't want the whole world to see, including your mom, your boss, your future children, your Rabbi, or your priest. It is really a good idea to have a separate account profile for professional purposes so that potential employers don't see any negative postings or pictures. This could negatively affect your potential as a job seeker or as a current employee.

A studio, called Reel FX, posted this tip in Figure 4.3 about the hiring process on Facebook on January 9, 2013.

ONLINE FORUMS

Becoming active on forums such as Creativecrash.com, Conceptart.org, Cgchannel.com, and Area.autodesk.com can be a great resource for not only networking but for feedback on your work and pointers from professionals. Most of the software companies have specific communities and forums geared toward their product, and you can also find tutorials and shared information on those sites.

This industry is filled with people who are grateful for all the help that they received on their journey and are more than willing to help those who ask.

> The currency of real networking is not greed but generosity.
>
> Keith Ferrazzi

Reel FX University (RFXU)

Tomorrow we are doing a Reel Review where members of the artist management team and two (or more) senior level animators view all of the reels that have been submitted by those who have applied for a position with our studio. Given production demands on the animation crew these are usually done over a lunch hour. So, tomorrow Artist Management and two "Turkey" Lead animators will review the 160+ reels that have been submitted since the latest job posting went up last Thursday afternoon. The reels will appear on a large screen and the Leads will tell us when they have seen enough to know whether or not the applicant has the right stuff.

They usually do not give notes, its more of a PASS/FAIL situation.

The 10 Second Rule is in full play. Keep in mind we have an hour to get through 160+ reels so rarely do we look at an entire reel. We will on occasion; when the reel is very-very good and then again when the reel is very-very bad. This time constraint is why it is SO IMPORTANT for applicants to put their best animation right up at the head of the reel!

Like · Comment · Share · 👍2 💬1 · 6 minutes ago · 🌐

👍 2 people like this.

 Reel FX University (RFXU) I worked for a while at a studio where we did Reel Reviews in a common area – any animator who wished could weigh in on the reel being viewed. This may seem harsh but during one of these sessions an animator saw his shots on another animator's reel. The applicant had claimed another artist's work as his own. That was a career killing move.

2 minutes ago · Like

Figure 4.3 Facebook Post on January 9, 2013, by Reel FX University
Source: https://www.facebook.com/pages/Reel-FX-University-RFXU/200141175201

I have even known people to post their demo reel for feedback, only to get hired. I'd say that's a pretty great outcome for socializing on a forum. So find a forum where your work aligns. Don't just ask questions. Try to answer some, too. Be helpful when you can. Begin paying it forward now.

TIPS FROM INDUSTRY PROFESSIONALS

The following tips were submitted to the anonymous survey. All suggestions and responses come from people who are currently working in the animation industry.

QUESTION: WHAT IS THE BIGGEST MISTAKE AN APPLICANT CAN MAKE WHEN APPLYING?

- Biggest mistake? Not having done their homework about the company they are applying to.
- Do not plagiarize. Give credit where it is due.
- Don't tell a lie or show someone else's work on your reel.
- Don't have a bad reel, and don't continuously e-mail.
- Terribly formatted résumés are a big mistake.
- Big mistake if they apply to a position that does not match their skillset.
- Any form of arrogance usually backfires ... For example, if one acts as if he/she has won the job before or even during the interview process, then that particular applicant typically does not get the job. Humility and respect are very important!
- Biggest mistakes: (1) Being overly pushy in correspondence. (2) Having a poorly put together reel and portfolio. (3) Using too many buzzwords in the résumé.
- As I don't take part in the hiring process at the studio I work at, I will make some mentions of mistakes and issues I've seen when looking at portfolios, business cards, résumés, and webpages: (1) Typos: One of the biggest mistakes I've ever seen gets made the most often. For the love of all things good, have someone read over your materials. As many friends as you can. Your mom, your friendly neighbor. Anyone. I used to work in a retail position (arts related) before a studio hired me, and there was a public postings board where people would post their flyers/business cards and links to portfolios/linked in/webpages and art-related material. Nothing made me feel more embarrassed for a person than a ridiculously simple and easy-to-avoid typo on a business card or

> The true secret of giving advice is, after you have honestly given it, to be perfectly indifferent whether it is taken or not, and never persist in trying to set people right.
>
> Henry Ward Beecher

portfolio flyer. Business cards with the word "address" misspelled, or a flyer with a whole paragraph was duplicated on the center portion of a tri-fold paper were something that could have been easily avoided. (2) Make sure if you send someone to your portfolio or webpage or e-mail, that you give them the right address, and that the page is actually up and running. Nothing stinks more than going to someone's portfolio address and they've let the hosting or domain registration lapse, or something is wrong with the coding. Also make sure those pages have some sort of contact such as an e-mail address. And don't use bizarre e-mails like "superbunnybutt28@suchandsuch.com." Have something somewhat recognizable. You can be funny and clever but make sure people can type your address in easily or can identify whom they are e-mailing. Oh, and avoid using Papyrus font.

- Don't apply for a job you're not qualified for. Like if you're a modeler but apply for a job that requires you to be a generalist.
- In my opinion, there are not many mistakes that can be made unless the reel is really off the mark. The reel should be easily accessible online and keep the e-mail brief. Long e-mails are lame and not needed. There are only three things you need to say: your URL, availability and your contact, and be polite. I always add "I hope all is well."
- Over branding their materials with "so and so productions" or "Joe Schmoe Animation Company."
- Biggest mistake: not sounding interested in the job. We often get people applying for positions they feel are beneath them and sound too big for the job. Example: "I was a CG supervisor on this commercial for this small studio, therefore I should be the sup at your extremely large feature animation house," or "I went to X for school and therefore I think I am above an entry-level position." I have yet to see one of those people hired.
- Stealing work from another person and claiming you did it is a big mistake. This industry is small, and you will never get away with it. When you do get called out (I have caught a couple people showing work I did), your reputation will be hurt. Often it can be one person that can keep you from being hired if they know you try to take credit for someone's work or are lying about their contribution.
- Begging for a job, while not having the necessary skills for it, is a big mistake.
- Biggest mistakes: (1) Overstating qualifications, like being an expert at everything, or VFX supervisor/art director credits on small or student

projects, and so on; (2) Not having a specialization, generalists have their place, but most large studios want a focus, not putting one confuses recruiting.

- (1) Wanting to wear too many hats: that is, "I'm a modeler/animator/ rigger/fx artist." (2) Being too eager (being humble and willing to work is good but it's nice to see that a candidate respects their own time/ talent). (3) Providing too many work examples (bad and good) instead of fewer good examples. (4) Being overconfident (confidence is great but it's also good to be humble).

- A poor portfolio. When they looked at mine, they picked just three of my projects at random off of my website and watched the animation from those. If any of them happened to be my weaker animations, I'd be sunk because they didn't look at anything else.

- The biggest mistake an applicant can make is to not include their contact information with their application. If we can't contact you, we can't hire you.

- (1) Calling back is not recommended. You can reapply again later. (2) It helps to apply for a position that matches your qualifications.

- Not applying. Contact every company you can.

- Adding too much to their résumé and portfolio.

- Not understanding their own strengths in regard to animation abilities and how those can fit into the studio's needs and help to improve the overall quality of the product.

- Not sending a reel. Not playing up your technical strengths.

- Not making the application/demo reel clear and to the point.

- Not being direct enough. Timid will get you nowhere.

- Not have a demo available.

- (1) Not putting your best work first on the reel. A good animator is noticeable in the first 30 seconds. So is a bad one. (2) Not being humble in interviews. No one wants to work with someone cocky, even if they're a great prospective otherwise. (3) Personal pet peeve is typos in a résumé, "especially" one that lists attention to details as a job skill. Also, just don't ever put "attention to details" as a job skill. We'll just assume you pay attention to the details by the way you present yourself.

- In a few cases, applicants have mentioned that they'd like to do the job offered but then would really like to move into a different field. In most people's minds this is supposed to come off as showing a desire for growth and a willingness to learn and adapt. From the perspective of the employer, all it really told us was that we'd have to be looking to fill this position again in the near future. The desire to get your foot in the door and move up into a position that you really want can be a great thing, but it's perhaps best to not mention it too directly in the initial interview.

- Having an "I know everything" attitude ... as well as not really knowing what they would like to do (TD vs. Anim vs. Modeler vs. Texure artist).
- Not addressing questions more directly. Volunteering information.
- Typos on résumé or shot breakdown, demo reel too long (put your best first), music on reel is ok—but make sure it's subtle and check the levels. Not following up at all is a big mistake. Also try to find someone other than jobs@blahcompany to send your application to.
- Not reading instructions. For example, if you are required to submit a demo reel of 30 seconds with no sound, make the necessary adjustments to fit their requirement ... this could be a test if you can follow instructions or not.
- Making contact too often and seeming desperate. Making a demo reel that is too long or has work that doesn't fit the job they are applying. Applying for a job they are not qualified for.
- Lie.
- With HR, it's generally the catch alls, putting a picture on your résumé, spelling mistakes, personal information that does not pertain to your job qualifications, and so on. With the animation directors, it is misrepresentation of your work or skill level. Always be honest in your work and your contribution to the shot/scene/animation on your reel. Some others have personal hang-ups, some don't like rendered shots, some don't mind it, that sort of thing. Sound on your reel is really all over the place as well. In my experience though if you don't have any lip sync in a shot, most animators don't want a sound track. However, if your work is representative of the position's skill level that you are applying for, most people will get an animation test at the least.
- Only using the Internet to apply for jobs. Also not comparing your portfolio to professionals and not gearing a part of their portfolio to a specific company.
- Using a form e-mail and not changing the name of the company they are applying too. Seen more times than I care to remember.
- Demo reel too long. Not finding out about the job first; that is: students see the position of tech animator and apply for it, because they think they will be able to transition into being an animator. When they send

an e-mail, they think that they will get a reply right away. The best way to think about it is if you send an e-mail, don't expect to get a reply ever or at least a month later.

- My comments pertain more to the interview process ... there aren't many mistakes I can think of when literally applying (short of sending materials to the wrong location or something). After that, watch out for: Being too generalized (larger companies hire for specific roles, though a few highly developed focuses can be fine). Acting overly confident (arrogant) or underconfident (timid or insecure). Being unprepared (unwilling/unable to answer questions about work/experience/the job applied for).

- Biggest mistakes an applicant can make when applying: (1) Lying or misrepresenting yourself on your reel. Don't put work on your reel that isn't yours, and don't say you did something, or can do something, if you can't. (2) Failing to properly edit and proofread your demo reel, résumé, cover letter, and other application materials. Your reel is only as good as your weakest piece. If you have misspelled words or poor grammar on your résumé/cover letter, it won't matter how good your work is.

- Not having enough talent.

- The applicant is unfamiliar with our studio. We're not just looking for talent; we're looking for talented people who want to work "here."

- Listing software and specific skills when applying to a smaller studio. Small shops look for generalists who are willing to do anything on any application.

- Exaggerating their capability with required software.

- Not knowing their audience or whom they're applying to. For example, applying to the animation department of a feature animation studio and having modeling on their reel.

- Assuming that we are interested in what we can do for him/her.

QUESTION: WHAT IS THE MOST IMPORTANT ADVICE THAT YOU WOULD GIVE TO POTENTIAL APPLICANTS?

- To not lose hope and to continue applying with an open mind.

- Be confident in your talent, be able to take criticism. If you do not succeed the first time, take the advice you get and work on it. Apply again. Either it will become clear that you are spinning your wheels or you will impress recruiters with your drive.

> Everything we hear is an opinion, not a fact. Everything we see is a perspective, not the truth.
>
> Marcus Aurelius

- If you don't get in the first time—apply again when your demo reel is updated. I am working at a studio that was one of the first I applied to. Even with a contact (friend) there, I was not interviewed with my first reel. I continued to stay up all night doing any freelance work and working on my demo reel, and 6 months later I applied again and got a job.
- Never stop working on your reel.
- If you have a dream company that you want to work in, do whatever you can to show off your skills to them in an appropriate setting. If a company is throwing any public event, jump in as fast as you can even if you have to crash the party. Try to impress as many industry people as you cannot just with your talent but ESPECIALLY with your attitude.
- Try to bring something of value to the hiring manager or interviewer. In other words, rather than appearing needy in an obvious way, appeal to the hiring manager's self-interests. An easy way to do this is to be grateful and complimentary without seeming obsequious. A written/ mailed thank-you note is also nice. And if you win the job, offer to take the hiring manager to lunch, or at least buy him, or her, a coffee some time ... Everyone likes to feel appreciated, and that goes double for the folks in charge!
- Keep it together. Keep yourself cool. Be prepared. Get advice from others and have them look over your stuff, especially if they are friends already working in a similar field. Although you don't have to take their suggestions, it never hurts to ask. And mind manners. Say thank you to everyone you encounter. Be clear, and be enthusiastic. I've seen people drop off applications to places with a rolled up résumé, and a shrug. That'll get you nowhere fast.
- Be versatile and want to learn new things. Also be yourself in a professional manner.
- Networking is the most important thing you can do when you're starting out. I could write a book on this, it's that important. Keep every contact you can. If you get an actual reply (from a human address) from any studio, keep it and use it appropriately. I divide initial success into 3rds, It's 1/3 skill, 1/3 luck, and 1/3 personality. You have to have at least two of the three to get a start if you're not exceptional coming out of school, once you're in, it's up to you and your work ethic. Never stop networking.

- Lead with your best work. Know the studio/group you are applying to. Be funny and personable! Lots of people have technical qualifications, but we care much more about a good personality fit.
- Be humble, be excited, and be yourself.
- Don't give up or assume you are going to work for a large studio right away and work on the best projects. When starting, keep working on your experience and skills. Keep learning and take on new experiences if you get the chance. Having built up a good amount of skills will make your application stronger to apply at a bigger studio. Also, save your money when you do find work. The industry has changed over the years and finding stable work is very hard, and you will need money between jobs. Studios will not keep people when there is no project to work on unless you perhaps have a skill or seniority that they can't risk letting you go. You will be moving around to find work so be prepared to pick up and move across the globe if it's the only option you have. Be watchful of how you are getting paid and if the person or studio that is paying you has the money. If they don't have the money, then get out right away.
- Be clear as to what you want to do with your career. Apply for a particular position, not all of them.
- Have a Vimeo reel, 1–2 minutes long. You'll be hired by your weakest work on that reel, so edit accordingly. Get a cell phone number in the area you're looking.
- Realize your talents and focus your reel on your strong suit. Show your best work and be able to explain your artistic/technical choices. Expect to earn your position and right to work on desired tasks. Remember that despite its creative elements, animation and visual effects are also a business.
- Make sure you put your best work out there and leave everything else out. Make sure you're getting paid adequately for your work. There are a lot of companies that want free or super cheap labor. That being said don't ask about salary until you're pretty much hired (asking for it too early can be a deterrent because it might just look like you're applying because you're desperate for money, not because you can offer something to them). Finally, research the company as best you can. Get the name of the person you're supposed to address the cover letter to. Find out what they're looking for, what their style is, and what you can

best give to them. It's a hard thing to do and not all companies are easy to research, but do your best.

- Be concise and specific. A demo reel should showcase the best of your abilities: you have one chance to catch my attention.
- Keep in touch and apply often.
- Best shots up front. Shorter reel of best work is better. Tutorials aren't impressive. Create your own stuff; make it look as professional as possible.
- Make sure your reel fits the specific position. Make a tailored version of it for that job.
- Be yourself!
- Keep everything clear and concise. From your cover letter to the actual demo reel. Only show your best stuff, even if it only adds up to 30 seconds or so.
- Show only your strongest work on your reel. Play up your strengths and mention the specific technical skills/software that you bring to the table.
- Sell yourself on what you do and only show your best work.
- Make sure your best work is at the front and dont put anything mediocre in just to make it look like you have more stuff.
- Make a demo that stands you out. If it does not wow me, your résumé will not even be reviewed.
- Be honest about your experience, be humble in your interview, be yourself, and have a kick-ass reel and someone will hire you!
- For the Interview: For the love of god, just be who you really are. Don't give answers you think people just want to hear back as if it's a puzzle with only one right piece. Your ability as an artist will get you 90% of the way there but being a good fit for the team is also important. Every studio has its own philosophies of operation on things such as how strict or loose they are in their work environment, and not everyone is a perfect fit for every place. For the Reel: USE SUBTLE MUSIC OR NONE AT ALL. Nobody is going to judge you based on your musical interests and more often than not the music feels more invasive, distracting or down right annoying than it does cool. If you are applying for a specifically titled job, such as, "Environment Animator" keep your reel focused to pieces that represent that and save the things that show extended ability for the end or as extra material you can bring to an interview.

- Stay positive, be proud but not too proud of your work: always be open to criticism.
- Research the company. Find out what their vision is. Find out if they have comprehensive goals that enable them to construct a realizable mission statement.
- Move to a place where there are plenty of companies and you will have more opportunity for work. Most companies are not going to hire someone from out of the area for an entry-level position. Smaller houses may want you to start the next day. Make sure your talents and skills come through clearly from your résumé and reel. If you're just "ok" at something, don't include it. Always be polite in e-mail and phone calls—don't harass anyone. Know your labor laws! When negotiating a contract, make sure you have a clear understanding (and written confirmation) of your rate, and how you will be paid for overtime, weekends, and holidays.
- Polish your demo reel as best as you can and do the necessary research about the company you are applying for.
- Don't give up or be discouraged after a few months or a year even. Keep working on your stuff and try to have a new piece done every month. You never know if the same company may ask if you have any more stuff a month after applying. This is more likely to see if you have still been animating after school or since your last job.
- Be confident, know what you can do, and talk to them like peeps not like bosses.
- Be honest about your work. That is it. A number 1.
- Be specific to what you want to do and only show that. You can expand your expertise after you're hired.
- Quality over quantity. Only show your best work and be honest with yourself about your skill level. Many applicants with little skill expect to be hired and paid top dollar.
- Know what they're looking for and how to sell yourself. Read and re-read job posting. Try to come up with specific examples that qualify you for each point. Not only do you want to sell yourself as someone qualified for the job, but someone who people WANT to work with.
- If you are in school, look around your class and think really hard, are you in the top 10% that will be getting a job at a high-end company?
- Especially starting out, most places will of course question your lack of experience. It's always a risk to "vet" someone with no prior experience by bringing him or her into the middle of an expensive production.

You need to make this risk seem less to them. I would be prepared to sell your skills, your work ethic, your collaborative nature, your personality, and so on. By "sell" I don't mean lie or hopelessly exaggerate, I mean have real examples that demonstrate that you would be ready to work in a professional production team. Beyond that, apply for positions whose requirements match your skills. Your résumé/reel/portfolio will be all anyone knows of you at first and will need to convince the company you're worth contacting. After that, it's about demonstrating that you have the knowledge you claim and a personality people will actually want to work with day in and day out. If I could pick the three most important traits I respond to when interviewing people, they would be open-mindedness, honesty (authenticity), and above all enthusiasm.

- Be enthusiastic. Be persistent. Be honest, both with the world and with yourself. Know that you will never be done with your reel, you should always be adding new things to it.

- Make a killer demo reel and know the company you are applying to, if possible get inside information.

- (My experience is animation-specific) If you get a follow-up, research the studio. Know why you want to work "there." You are selling yourself, but if the studio is following up, they want to sell themselves to you, too. If possible, tailor your reel to the type of work you seek. Emphasize movement (action) animation for game development, performance (acting) for cinematics/film. Reel basics: Include only your best work, and keep the best of the best at the beginning and end. Keep it brief, and link/direct to additional content. For phone or onsite interviews, have questions you'd like to ask. Interviewers are ready to answer. Interviews are two-way, and, as an interviewer, there's nothing worse than trying to fill time with an applicant. For game development, expect to be interviewed by multiple disciplines (design, engineering/programming, art, animation). In the interview, be confident, but don't be afraid to admit that you don't know something. Better to say, "I don't know" than to pretend.

- Be open to any position and don't anticipate being a specialist or character animator out of school.

- It helps to know someone in the company as a referral.

- A candidate's reel usually speaks for itself. So have the best possible quality of animation on a reel. Then, just be nice and personable in your interview if you get one.

- Listen and answer the questions truthfully.

QUESTION: IS THERE ANYTHING ELSE YOU'D LIKE TO SHARE TO POTENTIAL APPLICANTS ABOUT THE JOB HUNT PROCESS?

- Remember to say please and thank you. Working in a large studio requires people skills.
- Be proactive on art forums and develop a good online reputation. Don't hoard your knowledge. Help other artists in need. Studios most often hire people from word of mouth, so the more connections you have the easier your chances are to find out about potential job opportunities that aren't posted online.
- Have a backup career in mind. Understand the politics of what your industry is going through: tax incentives, out sourcing, and so on.
- Be nice to everyone, even when not on the hunt for a job.
- Keep trying and keep updating your work. Your portfolio gets better all the time. Put some time into keeping the new and better stuff in, and moving older, weaker work out.
- Keep pushing through. Even though it can be tough out there, you need to know that there is a job for you. It may take you a while to get your dream job but in the meantime keep practicing and keep applying.
- If you're exceptional, the path will be created in front of you, but if you're like me and only mediocre at best (when I came out of school), then you have work to do. Take whatever you can at first, get in the door and learn. Make contacts. Keep working and be patient. I reworked my animation reel for a year after I graduated from SCAD, and I moved out to CA without a job, finally find one at Digital Domain moving boxes and changing light bulbs. I did that for a year and half making $10/hr. It was so hard to live in LA on that budget, but I met so many amazing contacts and harassed anyone (managers, artists, HR, and producers) that would let me to critique my reel. They tore it up, key frame by key frame for a year and half. I'd have a brand new reel every 3 months to show them and incorporated as many of the directions that so many of them gave me as I could. It was really hard, but little by little I became a better animator. Finally, all my mentors on the same reel after a year and half said "hey, this isn't bad, you're getting better." I knew that was a victory and sent it out immediately. Got my first job at a very little game company and never looked back. I returned to DD 6 years later as an animator after working for almost every studio in Santa Monica and Venice on some great shows with great people. I kept meeting people and kept working, always had a good attitude even when I was changing light bulbs. I attribute that to why so

> Never give up on a dream just because of the time it will take to accomplish it. The time will pass anyway.
>
> Earl Nightingale

many people were willing to help me along the way. Now, still having generous mentors, I am more of a generalist doing lighting, animation and fx for a very cool little studio on commercials. Never quit if you start out like me because you can make it if you want to. And enjoy it, it's your life.

- Reach. You may not have ALL the qualifications a group is looking for, but the good jobs are looking for people to grow and flourish. If you're going for hired gun contractor positions, skills tend to trump all. Lastly, don't give up. We have contacted people years after interviewing them if we were impressed.

- Be patient. Especially students. Understand that so much of the hiring process is out of your control. It doesn't matter how well you do in an interview, sometimes the company has already offered the position to someone else when you are being interviewed and you are just there in case they say "no." So much of it is just being in the right place at the right time.

- Times have changed in this industry, and it is not like it was 10 years ago. The work is shorter and cheaper, less frequent. Competition for jobs is harder, but will be easier as you get more experience over time. A lot of experienced guys in the field are leaving because of the instability or have to consider other work if they want to stay in the area and have a family. Keep working on your skills and take on new challenges often so you don't get pinned down.

- Build your network of friends and co workers ... this will be your biggest asset.

- Contact alumni or friends of friends at prospective studios you are interested in, be polite and ask for their advice, different places have different paths inside.

- Networking is a big, big plus. Also, try to carry business cards and an electronic portfolio (or at least a demo reel) on you. Seriously, you never know when you'll find a job opportunity. I was picked up as an intern for Humoring the Fates Animation studio when I was at Barnes and Noble. I happened to be there working on my portfolio for a change of environment, and the Head Animator happened to be there for leisurely book shopping. When he saw my portfolio, he asked me some general questions about animation. Having no idea who he was, I chatted with him and showed him my work. I was invited to come to the studio for an interview a month later. I've also picked up freelance jobs at Best Buy and Kinkos, while I was there for unrelated reasons. People don't want to search far and wide for the perfect worker, especially clients and small companies. They want someone they can trust, who they can be referred to or whom they feel they already "know" beyond a résumé or computer screen. Always be prepared. A smart phone or iPad is perfect for it. Finally, keep in touch with your colleagues and don't be afraid to do cheap or free internships while you're getting yourself started. This can help others in your field get to know your talents and work ethic, build your portfolio, and help you get real paying jobs in the future.

- Know the company you're applying for and cater your application toward their needs. We're small, so a generalist is more important to us than a specialist. That may not be the case for a larger, diversified studio.
- Make sure your résumé is targeted to the job you are applying for. It should be short and use more lists than sentences. Use a Chrono-Functional style with a table format, dates by year not month. Use powerful language without repetition. A page is fine for an entry-level position. Save your letters of rejection to prove to yourself you don't give up. Stay positive. Research the company well and know what their assets and weak points are. Use this knowledge to your advantage. Listen and never interrupt. Point out positive aspects of the company that make you want to stay there as an employee for the long term.
- Don't give up. Patience and persistence are key.
- Do not give up.
- The games industry in general is going through an interesting shift, with major publishers and developers scaling down, and indie groups spawning frequently. But, there are opportunities that continuously creep up, so don't get discouraged, and be open to opportunities you wouldn't have previously considered. You may learn something about yourself.
- It's brutal. Keep jumping through all the hoops until someone bites.
- Keep working and improving.
- Make sure you love what you do. It will show through in your work and the way you talk about the job to the employer.
- Be outspoken with your work and talents, the résumé will speak after.
- Sometimes it seems like the only way to get a job in this industry is to already have one. It's just not true. The HR guys are putting the "ideal" candidate description in the job listing, but if you've got the reel and the personality, they're not going to hold lack of experience against you. Keep trying and don't expect to start at the top. Not everyone gets to work on Dragon Age as his or her first gig. That being said, apply to the Dragon Age team if they're hiring.

- The industry is tight on jobs these days! Don't let that discourage you. What it means is that you are only going to get back what you put in. (If you are in school) Be one of the people who is at the labs for 12–14 hours a day to hone your talent. Every college class has a group of people that know each other because they are the ones always working on projects. They are an elite bunch with open membership, all you have to do is put the time in, and it gives you an incredible edge for the future. These are the people who have the highest percentage of job offers right out of college, and part of this business is whom you know. You might not be one of the lucky ones to get a job right out of the gate but knowing someone who does can be invaluable.
- Be persistent, and if you are a freelancer, don't be afraid to bug producers. That's why they are there.
- Be professional—especially during telephone or Skype interviews. Make sure the interviewers are not seeing anything that gives a bad impression, or diverts their attention ... enabling them to draw the wrong conclusions.
- Don't be picky for your first job—take anything you are qualified for. Just get in the door and you will find that your network in the business will expand quickly and you will have a much easier time finding the next position.
- Never give up.
- Keep working on your craft, always!!!
- Stick with it. Be persistent. Some of my friends took years before landing their first big feature animation contract. Others got them right away. Networking helps some. Also, be honest and open with yourself about where you want to be in your field. For example, a video game animation reel will be set up differently than a feature film reel. Having a focused reel is more beneficial than a general reel.
- Keep only great things in your portfolio get rid of anything not to the highest standard even if you only have two or three pieces.
- Don't over dress for interviews. It shows that you don't have a great deal of experience in this industry. This is not really a suit and tie industry and it immediately shows lack of experience.
- http://www.cgstudiomap.com/ Super helpful in locating studios. Don't get discouraged ... sometimes the job search is VERY discouraging. Once you get the job, work your ass off and get yourself noticed. Opportunities will end up finding you and people will want to work with you. Don't be a kiss ass. You'll gradually meet the people you need to meet if you make

friends first. Go out for drinks. Have a good time. Those friends you make might wind up knowing people that could help out your career. No one will want to introduce you to these people though if they don't like your company to begin with.

- Make sure your reel is really, really good.
- In my experience on both sides of the process, it's usually more straightforward than people think. A company has a position they are looking to fill with a qualified candidate. Lots of things can rule you out (experience, skill set, and eventually salary if your current pay is beyond the range of the position). I've had companies not call me back because of some detail they didn't like for a job I knew I was otherwise qualified for. Don't take it personally, in the end you want something that's the right fit for both sides or else it won't be a positive experience from the beginning. Keep at it, if you have the right skills the right opportunity will come up, and if you don't, then work on acquiring them in the meantime!
- Being a good artist who is even-tempered, reliable, and fun to work with is almost always desirable to an amazing artist who behaves like a jackass.
- Have information about every aspect of production but specialize in one. Get a hobby that you can create art work that can be a fall back plan.
- If at first you don't succeed, try and try again. I know I did.
- Flexibility is key, try not to act like a specialist if you are applying for an entry-level position.

It is important to remember, after you have read through all of these tips and suggestions, that this information is advice from a wide range of people who are working in animation, visual effects, or game studios, small or large, and everything in-between. Some of the advices here are contradictory; some of the advices apply to certain very limited situations. It is up to you to digest this information and choose what feels right for you.

> He is bad that will not take advice, but he is a thousand times worse that takes every advice.
>
> Irish Proverb

> Accept good advice gracefully as long as it doesn't interfere with what you intended to do in the first place.
>
> Gene Brown

ACTION LIST

BRAINSTORMING

- Identify where you would like to work.
- Choose your best three pieces to make your first demo reel.
- Scour the Internet job postings for job descriptions that meet your skills.
- Research the companies that interest you most.

CREATING

- Make a list of studios that you would like to apply to (cgstudiomap.com is a great place to begin).
- Create accounts on LinkedIn, Facebook, and Twitter. Connect to studios that interest you.
- Join an online forum or two and begin helping others or posting questions.
- Finish polishing your best three pieces so that you can assemble your demo reel.

CHAPTER 5

ASSEMBLING THE REEL

DEDICATED DEMO REEL DRIVE—THE EVER CHANGING DEMO REEL

When drawing, you spend most of your time getting proportion and perspective drawn correctly before you worry about shading. An artist doesn't start drawing at the top left corner and render the image perfectly as he works across the page. He takes the time to block out the overall image then continues to refine it until the final detail is placed. A similar approach should be done with a demo reel and animation portfolio. Consider your demo reel and animation portfolio an ongoing project. One that truly is never complete. Think of yourself and your work as a river: always changing, never stagnant.

As you continue to create newer and better pieces, add them to the dedicated hard drive and edit your reel. Depending on the quality of the existing pieces, you can either add them to the reel or replace something that may not reflect your new and improved abilities. You should always be updating your reel (and your resume for that matter), even when you are working. If you are working at a stable position, then updating two or three times a year is usually sufficient, in which case you will always be ready when an opportunity arises. If you are searching for work, your goal should be updating monthly with new and improved work.

CONTINUING EDUCATION

Just as you continue to develop your skills, so, too, should you continue to further your education. The technology in the animation industry is constantly changing. New software and tools continue to be developed. To keep a competitive edge, you should always be willing to learn. Watching tutorials online is a good place to start. Whenever possible, download trial versions or purchase the software used in the industry

I thought how lovely and how strange a river is. A river is a river, always there, and yet the water flowing through it is never the same water and is never still. It's always changing and is always on the move. And over time, the river itself changes too. It widens and deepens as it rubs and scours, gnaws and kneads, eats and bores its way through the land. ... Will the I that is me grow and widen and deepen? Or will I stagnate and become an arid riverbed? Will I allow people to dam me up and confine me to wall so that I flow only where they want? Will I allow them to turn me into a canal to use for they [sic] own purposes? Or will I make sure I flow freely, coursing my way through the land and ploughing [sic] a valley of my own?

Aidan Chambers, *This is All: The Pillow Book of Cordelia Kenn*

to keep your skills fresh. It used to be that companies would hire you and train you on the software. This still happens occasionally at larger studios, but you are more hirable if you already know (or are at least familiar with) the software a studio uses. Take more classes or get an advanced degree. The point is to always continue to improve yourself and your abilities.

Some online resources for continuing education that have been utilized by myself or someone I know include the following:

www.digitaltutors.com

www.gnomonschool.com

www.animationmentor.com

www.ianimate.com

ASSEMBLING

Putting together your first demo reel is actually quite simple.

1. Choose the best three pieces you have.
2. Save them to a dedicated hard drive.
3. Place a slate at the beginning and end with your name and contact information.
4. Assemble your best work in a nonlinear editor.
5. Export your reel.

The aim of education is to enable individuals to continue their education … (and) the object and reward of learning is continued capacity for growth.

John Dewey

Of course, there are many other things you can do to make the reel better, but these five items can be done quickly and efficiently and provide you with a starting point from which to spring.

The first thing you put on your reel is the absolutely best thing you have ever created. The first piece must impress the viewer or they will not look any further. Studios receive anywhere from ten to thousands of reel submissions a week. Make sure that the first thing they see grabs their attention in the first 10–15 seconds and makes them want to watch more. The second piece is your next best, and the last piece should be almost as good as the first. If they make it that far, this provides them with something to remember you by. Remember, quality, not quantity, is important. You will be judged by the worst piece on your reel, so don't put anything on your reel that isn't your absolute best work.

SLATE OR ANIMATED LOGO INTRODUCTION (4–5 SECONDS)

The first thing seen on your demo reel is a brief opening introduction or your best work followed by the opening. Some artists create an opening incorporated into a reel piece. At a minimum, you can put a slate that lasts for no more than 5 seconds. This can be something that showcases who you are and what you do, much like your business card as in Figure 5.1. You can create a 5-second, animated logo, so when designing your logo, you should design it with your demo reel opening in mind. In addition to your logo, you should include your contact information. Whatever you create, make it quick (3–5 seconds) and get on with it. Your contact information should also be at the end of your reel.

> Creativity is allowing yourself to make mistakes. Art is knowing which ones to keep.
>
> Unknown

Figure 5.1 Example Opening Slates From Various Reels

CONTACT INFORMATION

This may sound obvious, but you must put your contact information on your reel: your name, phone, e-mail, and what you do, that is, animator. Make sure your reel contents reflect what you say you do.

NONLINEAR EDITING (30 SECONDS TO 3 MINUTES)

When assembling your reel in a nonlinear editor, the main thing to remember is to keep it simple and clear. Refrain from using bizarre or cheesy transitions. Keep transitions between clips simple: use cuts, quick cross-dissolves, or wipes. Abstain from cutting up your pieces into 1- or 2-second-long clips to mix things up and cause the viewer confusion. Do not put anything you did from a tutorial. Never put someone else's work on your reel and claim it as yours. Your purpose is to show your best original work with clear information as to what you did in each clip. Your reel must be able to be frozen and advanced frame-by-frame because that is what is going to happen sometimes if the studio likes what they see.

Showing your thought process whenever possible is really great so that the studio can try to understand how you think. If you don't want to show this on the demo reel, you can show your thought process on a website. This can be done more easily when documenting your creativity as you go about creating your work, such as rendering out the individual passes needed for compositing or keeping various stages of animation playblasts. If not, you may need to backtrack and create the elements needed when putting together your reel.

Show initial ideas, sketches, drawings, and thumbnails. Show the reference you used and the research you did during development. More technical positions, like riggers, want to show demonstrations of how the rigs work. This can be done using software that will capture the computer screen as you navigate through features of how the rig controllers or scripting tools work. Be sure to choreograph what you will do and then speed up these recordings in a nonlinear editor, so that your work can be shown efficiently.

Other positions need to be creative for effectively putting together a demo reel. For example, the 3D Depth Artist can show examples of converted shots on a 2D reel by rendering into anaglyph or by showing the depth layer in the image breakdown. Splitting off the red channel with the wiggler in After Effects can "fake" the stereo, or freezing the shot on a frame and switching between the left eye and right eye for a few seconds reveals the stereo/convergence.

While there are many creative ways of presenting your work, the following ideas seem to be the most effective without being distracting:

1. Cuts can be used most effectively for a series of clips.
2. Split screen can be used for comparing one thing with another side-by-side. A variation on this idea can include a larger image of the finished

piece with an inset, like a picture-in-picture. A split screen is a great way of showing how you interpret sketches, storyboards, or concepts on one side of the screen and finished work on the other, or how your sketches, storyboards, or concepts were eventually realized into the final shot. Split screens are also a great way of showing a close-up detail of a section of the final image, such as a turntable of a model on one side of the screen with a detail of the same model on the other.

3. Cross-dissolve can be used when comparing something before and after or a finished render with a technical aspect. It can also be used with a buildup to show different stages to the finished image. Cross-dissolve can be used to compare the wireframe turntable of a model with the rendered textured model.

4. Linear wipe transition can be used when showing one element after another as you build up to the final finished image. Many compositors show a buildup between the "original" and "finished" plates of their work, and to great effect, using linear wipe transitions to create a shot buildup adding subsequent passes of the sequence to show the different "stages."

MUSIC AND TIMING

No one cares to hear music, really. They will not even turn the sound on. However, if they do happen to have the volume turned up and if they don't like your choice in music, they may not even watch the rest of your reel. If you do decide to use music, you should probably stick with something instrumental. It can be a good idea to actually cut your reel to a soundtrack, because it gives you a natural flow and rhythm that you might not have otherwise. It provides a rhythmical pacing to how your work is edited together. Use your networking skills to make friends with a sound designer or musician and ask them to create some music specifically for your reel. Perhaps you can barter some visuals that they may need in exchange.

LEGAL ISSUES WITH MUSIC

Demo Reels that are posted online on YouTube or Vimeo cannot have copyrighted music as part of the reel. If you are going to post a demo reel on your own website, you should be fine with using copyrighted music as the soundtrack, as long as you are not making money off the distribution of your reel and you credit the music at the end of your reel. However, this is a gray area, and an additional reason as to why you shouldn't have music on your reel.

TEXT OVERLAY

A good idea is to put what you did for each piece on your reel as an overlay at the bottom of the screen as in Figure 5.2. At any point the demo reel can be paused and it is clear what you did the shot without having to search through a breakdown shot list or resume.

Make sure that whatever font you use can be read easily. If you have text overlay on your video, separate the words from the background simply, perhaps using a white box behind black text or a black box behind white text. Remember, legibility and readability are the goals here. Stay away from drop shadows or other font effects as it makes the words very difficult to read. Limit any text overlay because you want the viewer to be looking at your work, not reading the whole time. Refer Chapter 1 for more information about font and font choices. Keep your font choice consistent with other fonts used in your portfolio and package design.

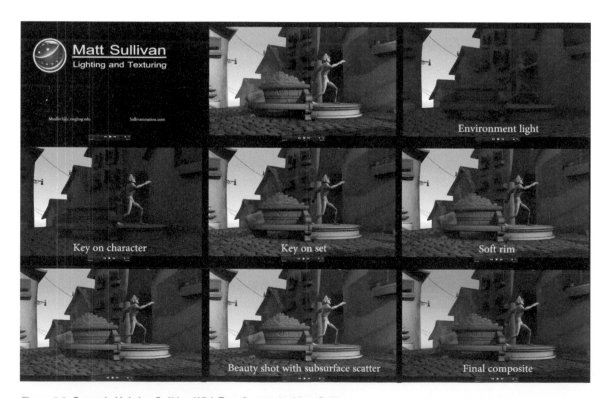

Figure 5.2 Example Lighting Buildup With Text Overlay by Matt Sullivan

DO's

Dedicate a hard drive for your demo reel.

Update your demo reel every 3 months with some new work.

Continue to create new and improved work.

Continue to learn new techniques and tools.

Put only your best work on your demo reel.

Show your thought process.

Place an easy to read text overlay to note what you did for each piece on your reel.

DON'Ts

Don't put anything except your best work on your demo reel.

Don't put any tutorials on your reel.

Don't forget to put your contact information on your reel.

Don't put anyone else's work on your reel and claim it as your own.

Don't use bizarre or cheesy transitions between clips.

Don't cut up a piece into smaller clips to mix things up and cause the viewer confusion.

Don't repeat the same piece in your reel.

Don't put color bars and a 2-pop cue.

Don't use music or sound, unless it is integral to what we are seeing on screen, such as a lip-sync.

Don't use copyrighted music if posting on Vimeo or YouTube.

When assembling a demo reel, I recommend using a nonlinear editor, such as Adobe Premiere or Final Cut Pro or a motion graphics and compositing software, such as Adobe After Effects or Nuke. Your project files along with original footage and images files, should be organized on a dedicated hard drive, or at the very least, a partition on a hard drive. This drive should be also backed up regularly to minimize the risk of lost data. The point of all of this is to make updating your demo reel and other materials more efficient.

TUTORIAL 5.1: ASSEMBLING A DEMO REEL IN ADOBE PREMIERE

1. If you haven't created a project folder already, make sure to do so now. You can create a folder structure like the one discussed in Chapter 3 or download the AnimationPortfolio folder structure on reelsuccess.com already created for you.
2. Place all your files in the appropriate folders, if you haven't done so already.
3. Open Premiere. Choose **New Project**. In the New Project dialogue box (Figure 5.3), choose your **Location** by navigating to where you would like to save your project files. (AnimationPortfolio > 06_DemoReel > NonLinear_ Editing if you are using the folder structure provided on reelsuccess.com.)

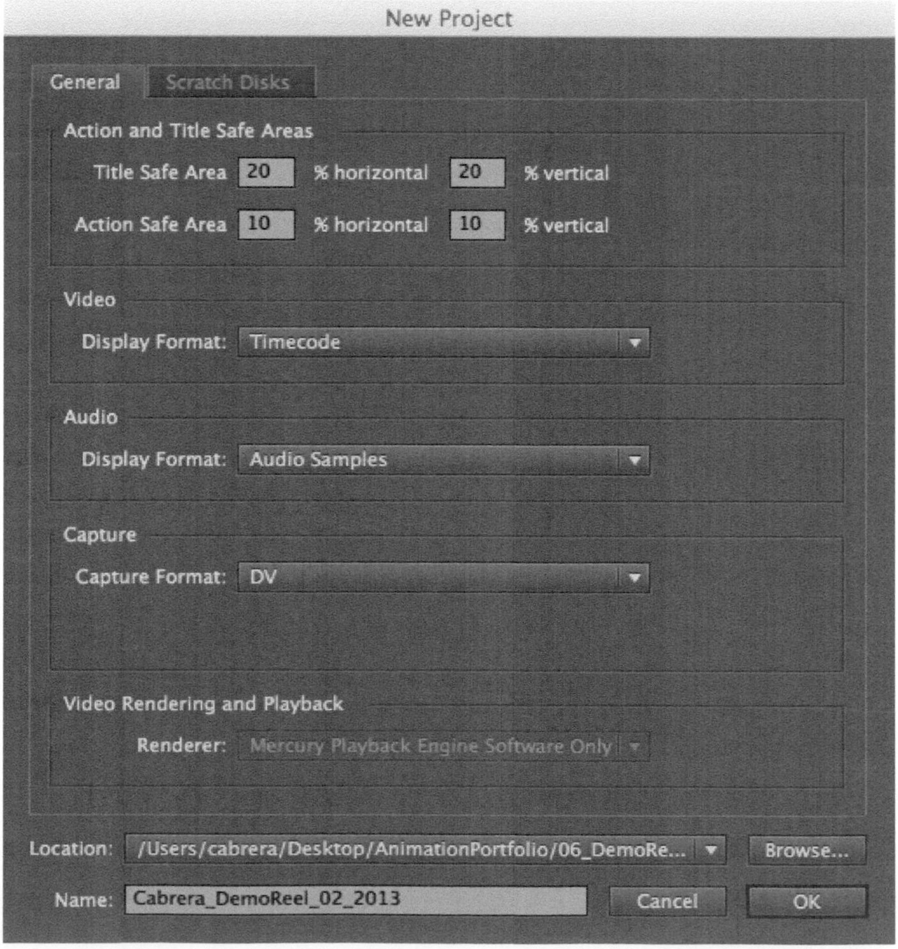

Figure 5.3 The New Project Dialogue Box

Name your project as well. I usually name my project with the date of the version in the filename: *Cabrera_DemoReel_02_2013*.

4. Choose a Sequence preset based on the video dimensions of your largest clip as in Figure 5.4. Ideally, all your clips should be the same size resolution or your reel may look odd. Remember that all your clips need to be at the same frame rate time base. HDV 720p30 or HDV 720p24 is a good choice, depending on at what size and rate you work.

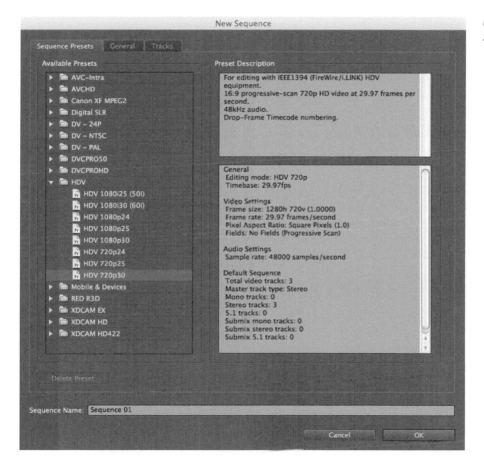

Figure 5.4 The New Sequence Dialogue Box

5. Import all your clip files. Go to **[File > Import]** and browse to find your clips. Be sure to include your Title Slate or opening animation.

6. Select the title slate or opening animation and then to add to your selection **hold down command on a mac or control on a pc and click** the clips in the order you want them to appear in the timeline.

7. Drag your selections into the Video1 track of the timeline.
8. Drag your title slate again at the end of your reel.

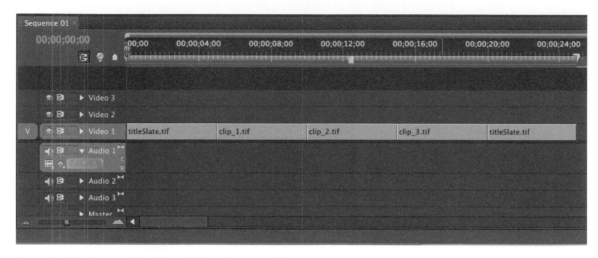

Figure 5.5 *The Sequence Timeline with Title Slate and Clips*

This completes a simple demo reel as in Figure 5.5. All clips are transitioned using a cut. If you want to add transitions, the following tutorials walk you through how to add those discussed in this chapter.

TUTORIAL 5.2: CREATING A SPLIT SCREEN IN ADOBE PREMIERE

1. Open your project in Premiere, if it is not open already.
2. To play both clips at the same time side by side, drag clip 2 into the Video 2 track directly above clip 1 in the Sequence timeline as in Figure 5.6.

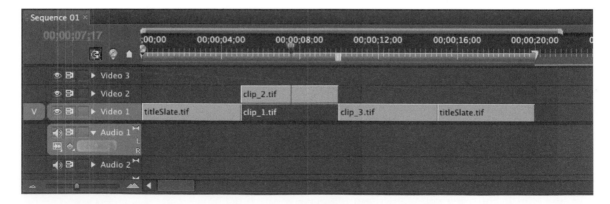

Figure 5.6 *The Sequence Timeline Window Showing the Location of the Clip 2 Above Clip 1*

3. In the **Effect Controls** window [**shift + 5**], adjust the scale of each video clip by:
   a. Select the clip in the timeline.
   b. Click on the little triangle arrow on the left of **Motion** in the **Video Effects** section of the **Effect Controls** window.
   c. Change **Scale** to **50.0** as in Figure 5.7.

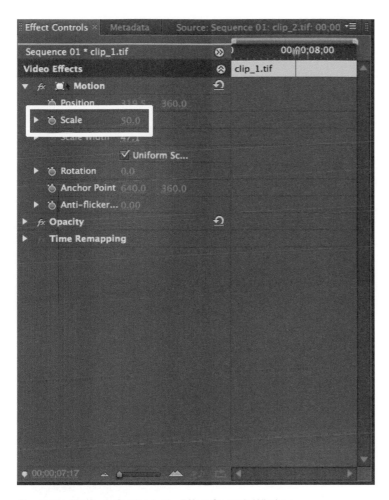

Figure 5.7 The Scale Setting in the Effect Controls Window

4. Click and drag clip 1 to reposition it to the left in the Program Monitor.
5. Click and drag clip 2 to reposition it to the right in the Program Monitor as in Figure 5.8.

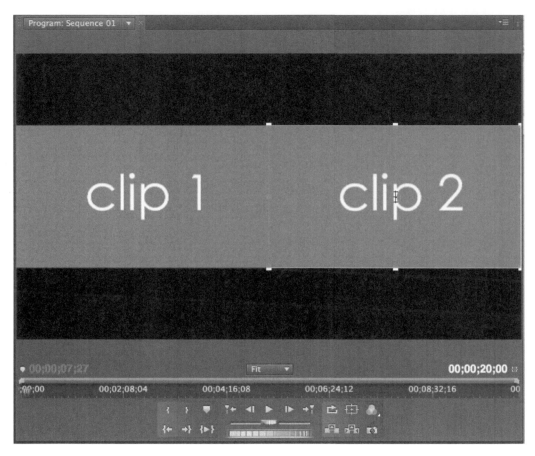

Figure 5.8 The Program Monitor Window

6. In the **Effect Controls** window [**shift + 5**], center each clip vertically by:
   a. Select the clip in the timeline.
   b. Click on the little triangle arrow on the left of **Motion** in the **Video Effects** section of the **Effect Controls** window.
   c. Change **Position** to **360.0** as in Figure 5.9 if working at a 720 vertical resolution (or half of your vertical project resolution.)
7. If you scrub through the timeline, you can preview the split screen.

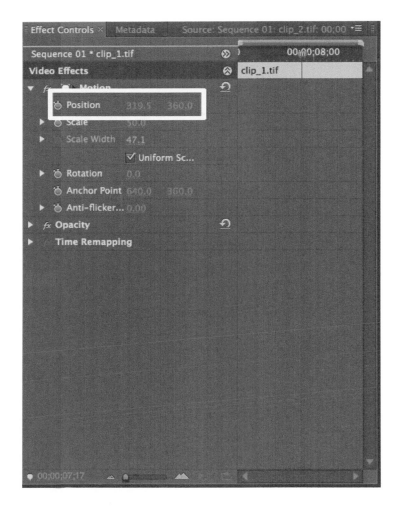

*Figure 5.9 The Position
Setting in the Effect
Controls Window*

TUTORIAL 5.3: CREATING A CROSS-DISSOLVE
IN ADOBE PREMIERE

1. Open your project in Premiere, if it is not open already.
2. Display your Effects window by going to: **Window > Effects** or pressing
   [shift+7] on your keyboard.
3. Scroll down and open the **Video Transitions** folder by clicking on the
   little triangle arrow on the left.
4. Scroll down and open the **Dissolve** folder by clicking on the little
   triangle arrow on the left as in Figure 5.10.

5. Click and drag the Cross Dissolve onto your timeline and in between the two clips as in Figure 5.11.

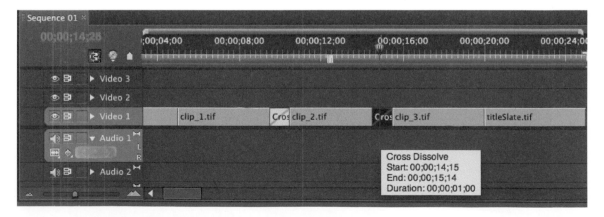

Figure 5.11 The Sequence Timeline Window Showing the Location of the Cross Dissolve Transition Between Clips

6. If you scrub through the timeline, you can preview the cross dissolve.
7. If you double click on the Cross Dissolve transition in the timeline, the Effect Controls window opens where the Duration and alignment can be adjusted, if necessary as in Figure 5.12.

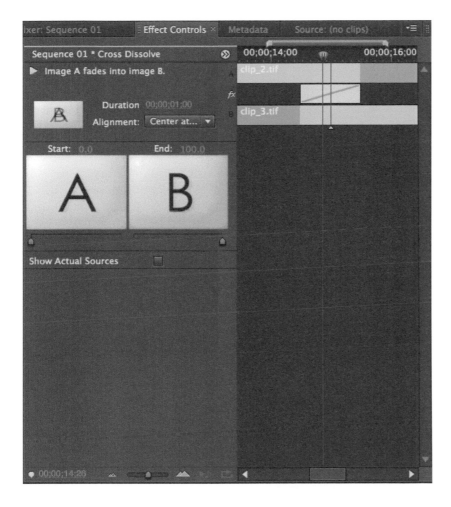

Figure 5.12 The Effect Controls Window

TUTORIAL 5.4: CREATING A LINEAR WIPE IN ADOBE PREMIERE

1. Open your project in Premiere, if it is not open already.
2. Display your Effects window by going to: **Window > Effects** or pressing [**shift + 7**] on your keyboard.

3. Scroll down and open the **Video Transitions** folder by clicking on the little triangle arrow on the left.

4. Scroll down and open the **Wipe** folder by clicking on the little triangle arrow on the left as in Figure 5.13.

Figure 5.13 The Effects Window Showing the Location of the Wipe Transition

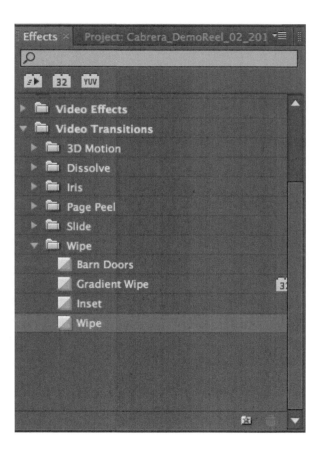

5. Clip 1 (located in the Video 1 track) will play first. Drag clip 2 into the Video 2 track directly above clip 1 in the Sequence timeline, trimming the beginning of the clip if necessary or offsetting the beginning of the clip so that there is overlap over clip 1 for the wipe transition to occur as in Figure 5.14.

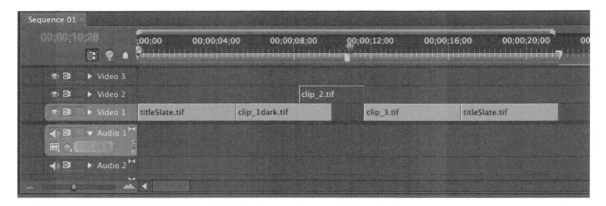

Figure 5.14 The Sequence Timeline Window Showing the Location of the Clip 2 Above Clip 1

6. Click and drag the Wipe transition onto your timeline and onto clip 2 as in Figure 5.15.

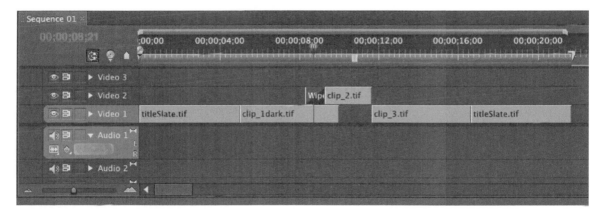

Figure 5.15 The Sequence Timeline Window Showing the Location of the Wipe Transition

7. If you scrub through the timeline, you can preview the Wipe.
8. If you double click on the Wipe transition in the timeline, the Effect Controls window opens where the Duration can be adjusted, if necessary, and a border can be added, or the direction of the wipe can be changed as seen in Figure 5.16.

Figure 5.16 *The Effect Controls Window*

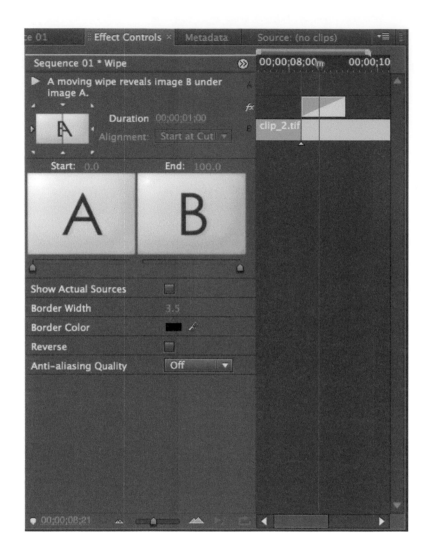

Sample Demo Reels and Video Tutorials on how to assemble a demo reel, create a split screen, create a cross-dissolve, and create a linear wipe can also be found on the website: www.reelsuccess.com using Premiere, After Effects, and Final Cut Pro.

CHAPTER 6

THE BREAKDOWN

Practically all great artists accept the influence of others. But ... the artist with vision ... by integrating what he has learned with his own experiences ... molds something distinctly personal.

—Romare Bearden

CLEAR INFORMATION

The breakdown is a list that specifies exactly what you have done on each clip shown. The purpose of the demo reel breakdown is so that the person watching knows what they are looking at and what your role was in its creation. Did you write the story? Do the layout? Do the modeling? How about the animation? Did you shade and texture? Did you render? Composite?

When someone views your reel, there should be no doubt in their minds as to what you have done on the pieces that they are seeing. You can overlay on the reel in the top or bottom corner what you have done and where it was done (company name, personal project, and school assignment). Another option would be to create a slate that displays this information before each clip on your reel. Be sure to also include a breakdown document so that the viewer can refer to it as they watch your reel.

This does not mean that you must have done everything that you show on your demo reel. In fact, it is great if you can show that you worked as a member of a team. Animation is a team sport. Studios complete projects with teams of people, so it is to your benefit to be able to show that you can play well with others. Just make sure that on your breakdown you list exactly what you have done and that what you did is absolutely clear.

In the corner of your reel, you can add numbers to each clip, which then corresponds with the items on the breakdown where your items are also numbered. If you have done everything in the shot, simply state so. Add a thumbnail image for each piece of the breakdown to make it easier for the person reading the information to identify which piece you are talking about.

GIVE CREDIT WHERE CREDIT IS DUE

> On the mountains of truth you can never climb in vain: either you will reach a point higher up today, or you will be training your powers so that you will be able to climb higher tomorrow.
>
> Friedrich Nietzsche

Credit those necessary, but don't promote anyone but yourself, unless you are working with your friends to try to help each other get jobs. In other words, if you worked as part of a team, declare only what you have done and state that you were part of a team, group project, or collaboration. Specific names aren't necessary in this situation. However, if you have used a rig that you have found online or another asset that you have been given permission to use, state the website or person who created it.

I once had a rigging student who stated credit information on the corner of their demo reel using text overlay: Model by Joe Smith, Animation by Gary Jones, and so on. When people watched it, the feedback was, ok well what did he do? Instead of stating what other people did, he should have stated what he did, such as, character rig, facial rig, and creature rig.

I also know someone who was contacted by a company, because they were interested in hiring them as a Lighting Artist. Imagine how embarrassed they were when they had to explain that the lighting was actually done by someone else on the project. The company actually then asked for that person's contact information.

PAGE LAYOUT

Design of the demo reel breakdown should be consistent with your portfolio package. Make sure to have your name and contact information on the page. You can utilize your letterhead as a starting point for this, and then layout your breakdown information accordingly on the page in an easy to read format.

Each clip in your demo reel should be listed with the following information:

Number and thumbnail image.

The month and year it was completed.

Length of clip (time code).

Title or description of piece.

Was it a group project, personal project, or a professional project? If this is a professional project, what company?

What did you do specifically? What were your responsibilities?

What software/tools did you use?

You can also add how long it took for you to complete the work seen in the clip.

Credit anyone if necessary.

The time it took for you to complete the work is something that, if you don't list it on the breakdown, will undoubtedly become a question during the interview process. If you decide not to list it here, it is good information to be aware of and know. Companies want to know not only what you are capable of creating but also how efficient you are as well.

Ideally, you can take your breakdown and make it into an interactive web page, where your process can be shown along with the final result.

SAMPLE DEMO REEL BREAKDOWNS

The following are varied examples of demo reel breakdowns.

The demo reel breakdown in Figure 6.1 is a good example to evaluate. We can note that Tonya has provided the following information about each clip of her demo reel:

- Number of piece.
- Name of piece.
- Description of what Tonya did for this piece.

As there are 17 pieces on her reel, numbering them was a good idea especially because thumbnail images are not available to help distinguish the pieces for the viewer. This demo reel breakdown is lacking some critical information and is not very helpful. Who does this breakdown belong to and how do we contact them? Some entries are just the title of the piece. Does that mean she did everything in that clip, or should I assume it's the same as a different entry, and which one? What tools did she use to create this?

Demo Reel Breakdown

1. Bait: Animation of the Moth (for this shot only, which appears in segments throughout my reel), created about half the textures for the set, UV mapping almost everything, lighting for the porch light, compositing the background, setting up, and managing renders
2. Bait: Same as above, plus Rigging the Bat
3. Bait
4. Anteater: Modeling, Rigging, Animation, Shader
5. Bait: Assisted in Rigging the Spider, implemented the Stretchy Spine and all of the expressions that control the spider and keep his eight shoulders from deforming badly, in addition to #1
6. Bat: Animation, Rigging
7. Ape: Rigging and Rig Demo using Windows Media Encoder
8. Bait
9. Dog: Rigging, Animation, UV mapping, and Shader/Texture
10. Centipede: Rigging Only
11. Bait: Same as #5, plus lighting for the Christmas and Flood lights
12. Glasses: Everything, Rendered in Mental Ray with Global Illumination and Final Gather
13. Minoan Villa: Everything, Rendered in Mental Ray with Global Illumination and Final Gather
14. Bait
15. Mini Cooper: Everything, Modeled with NURBS
16. Bait
17. Stir Crazy: Stop Motion, helped write and storyboard the story, helped build the set, built and animated puppet with blocks for neck, operated capture camera, editing and sound

Figure 6.1 Example Demo Reel Breakdown by Tonya Payne. Tonya is freelance animator for BreakAway Games, after working for them for 4 years as a full time staff artist (generalist). She is also an adjunct faculty member for Northwest Vista Community College

Tonya was hired in 2006. The competition today is getting fiercer. It is best to make reviewing your work as easy as possible for everyone involved.

The demo reel breakdown in Figure 6.2 is an ideal example to evaluate. In this single item from the demo reel breakdown of Benjamin Willis shown in Figure 6.3, we can note the following information:

- Thumbnail of piece.
- Name of piece.
- Length of piece.
- Description of why this piece was created and where.
- List of tools (software) used.
- Description of what Benjamin did for this piece.

//BENJAMINWILLIS
character animator

65 Lake Shore Rd.
Salem, NH 03079

http//:www.benjaminwillis.net
ben@benjaminwillis.net

Demo Reel Shot List:

Weight Test – 0:10
Short clip focusing on portraying weight through animation.

Tools Used: Maya 7

I only did the animation for this clip. Model and rig thanks to The Academy of Art College.

As Good As It Gets **Lip Sync** – 0:09
Short lip sync focused on acting and emotion.

Tools Used: Maya 7

I only did the animation for this clip. The audio is from the movie As Good As It Gets. Model and rig thanks to The Academy of Art College.

Quark – 1:21
Short film completed for Final Project 1 class at the Savannah College of Art and Design (SCAD).

Tools Used: Maya 5, Adobe Photoshop, Adobe After Effects

I did everything for this animation. This includes modeling, animation, rendering, compositing, sound design, character design, and story.

Amadeus **Lip Sync** – 0:13
Short lip sync completed during an independent study at SCAD, focusing on acting and emotion.

Tools Used: Maya 6

I only did the animation for this clip. The audio is from the movie Amadeus. Model, rig, and texturing done by Josh Burton.

The Potter – about 7:00
Short film completed with five other students while at SCAD. This was a collaborative project in which I assisted both areas of direction and animation.

Tools Used: Maya 6

I only did the animation for these shots. Model, rig, and texturing done by Josh Burton.

Figure 6.2 Example Demo Reel Breakdown by Benjamin Willis. Benjamin is an animator for Dreamworks Animation. His first job was working at Charlex as an animator on One Rat Short

Quark – 1:21
Short film completed for Final Project 1 class at the Savannah College of Art and Design (SCAD).

Tools Used: Maya 5, Adobe Photoshop, Adobe After Effects

I did everything for this animation. This includes modeling, animation, rendering, compositing, sound design, character design, and story.

Figure 6.3 Entry From the Demo Reel Breakdown by Benjamin Willis

The information is presented clearly. As there are only five pieces on his reel, numbering them was not necessary. The thumbnail images are helpful in distinguishing which piece the viewer is referring. His name and contact information are easy to find, because letterhead was used as the foundation for the breakdown.

The information is presented clearly and effectively in the demo reel breakdown of Joey Lenz seen in Figure 6.4. As there are only eight pieces on his reel, numbering them was not necessary, and the thumbnail images are sufficient to distinguish the pieces for the viewer. This demo reel breakdown has one major problem that needs to be addressed. Who does this breakdown belong to and how do I contact him? His name is listed for each piece, but his contact information is nowhere to be found.

In this item from the demo reel breakdown of Joey Lenz shown in Figure 6.5, we can note the following information:

- Thumbnail of piece.
- Name of piece.
- List of software (tools) used.
- Description of why this piece was created and where.
- List of what Joey did for this piece.
- List of what someone else did for this piece.
- Short description of why this piece was created.

In this example of the demo reel breakdown for Harrison Stark seen in Figure 6.6, the name and contact information are easy to find, because letterhead was used as the foundation for this breakdown, just as it was in the first example breakdown for Benjamin Willis.

With 11 pieces on his reel, numbering the thumbnails could have helped with the organization of the breakdown, especially since there are two columns. Having two columns could make the viewer somewhat confused as to which direction (horizontally or vertically) the next piece is listed. This demo reel breakdown is also lacking some important information, such as what tools were used.

In this item from the demo reel breakdown of Harrison Stark shown in Figure 6.7, we can note the following information:

- Thumbnail of piece.
- Name of piece.
- What Harrison did for this piece.
- What someone else did for this piece.

BREAKDOWN SHEET

Sci-fi Corridor, Software: Maya, Photoshop, mental ray, and Nuke

Responsibilities: Joey Lenz - modeling, layout, procedural/file-based texturing, animation, particle fx, lighting, and compositing
Camille Kuo - concept

The objective of this project was to gain a better understanding of moody environment lighting. With a lack of sci-fi in my current body of work, I wanted to try something different by creating a darker, dirtier piece.

Cell Phone, Software: Maya, Photoshop, mental ray, and Nuke

Responsibilities: Joey Lenz - modeling, texturing, animation, lighting, and compositing

I created an idealistic cell phone for a fake advertisement. The lighting setup for this piece was to focus on product visualization. Digital reflector boards were used to create the sharp, strong reflections seen within the surface of the cell phone model.

Telescope, Software: Maya, Photoshop, mental ray, and Nuke

Responsibilities: Joey Lenz - modeling, texturing, lighting, and compositing

This project was treated as a still-life study to challenge my artistic abilities by only using spot lights and to avoid software that renders indirect lighting effects.

Render Layers Setup Tool, Software: Maya and text editors

Responsibilities: Joey Lenz - coding

During the lighting/compositing stage, there are a lot of redundant tasks that have to manually be set up, like light linking, various render layers, and networks created in Nuke. Instead of repeating these actions, I created a few tools that automate them and shaves hours off my lighting/compositing workflow.

Hydrant, Software: Maya, HDRShop, Photoshop, Zbrush, Mudbox, mental ray, and Nuke

Responsibilities: Joey Lenz - modeling, motion tracking, procedural texturing, lighting, and compositing
Phil Liu - sculpting and texturing

To refine my live-action integration skills, I created a digital hydrant that matched the coloring and lighting of a real, motion tracked one.

Perceptions, Software: Maya, Photoshop, mental ray, and Nuke

Responsibilities: Joey Lenz - vfx supervision, animation, and compositing
Steve Lesniak - texturing, lighting, and compositing

This was one of several vfx shots I helped with for a senior film, *Perceptions*, directed by Rebekah Roediger. After a previous vfx team worked on it, we refined the shots based on the requests of the director.

Globe, Software: Maya, Photoshop, BodyPaint, mental ray, and Nuke

Responsibilities: Joey Lenz - lighting and compositing
Phil Liu - modeling and texturing

The focus of this project was projection texturing, challenging my artistic abilities by only using spot lights, and avoiding software that renders indirect lighting effects.

The Desolo Aura, Software: Maya, Vue, Photoshop, BodyPaint, Mudbox, mental ray, and Nuke

Responsibilities: Joey Lenz - concept, modeling, layout, procedural texturing, rigging, animation, particle fx, lighting, and compositing
Phil Liu - concept, finalized concept art, layout, file-based texturing, and matte painting

This was the most challenging visual effects project I have ever worked on. With just a team of two, making sure we could bring everything together, to making a cohesive design, to overcoming technical obstacles, and even faking perspective to create a grand sense of scale, was all an ambitious effort we managed to complete.

Figure 6.4 Example Demo Reel Breakdown by Joey Lenz. Joey is currently in school studying visual effects at the Savannah College of Art and Design

Hydrant, Software: **Maya, HDRShop, Photoshop, Zbrush, Mudbox, mental ray, and Nuke**

Responsibilities: Joey Lenz - modeling, motion tracking, procedural texturing, lighting, and compositing
Phil Liu - sculpting and texturing

To refine my live-action integration skills, I created a digital hydrant that matched the coloring and lighting of a real, motion tracked one.

Figure 6.5 Entry From the Demo Reel Breakdown by Joey Lenz

In this next example of the demo reel breakdown for Chris Jaser seen in Figure 6.8, the name and contact information are once again easy to find, because letterhead was used in this case as well. However, the layout for this breakdown is a little confusing, because it includes two versions of his reel, a short version and a long version, as well as a separate synopsis for a short film that he created. Repeated thumbnails and placing text that is too close makes the layout look cluttered and difficult to read. In this closer look at two of the items from the demo reel breakdown of Chris Jaser shown in Figure 6.9, we can see the awkwardness of the text as well as note the following information:

- Thumbnail of piece.
- Number of piece.
- Name of piece.
- Length of piece.
- List of software used.
- Description of what Chris did for this piece.

Creating different versions of the demo reel also requires the creation of different versions of your breakdown. It is more effective to keep them separate and not try to put them all together on one page.

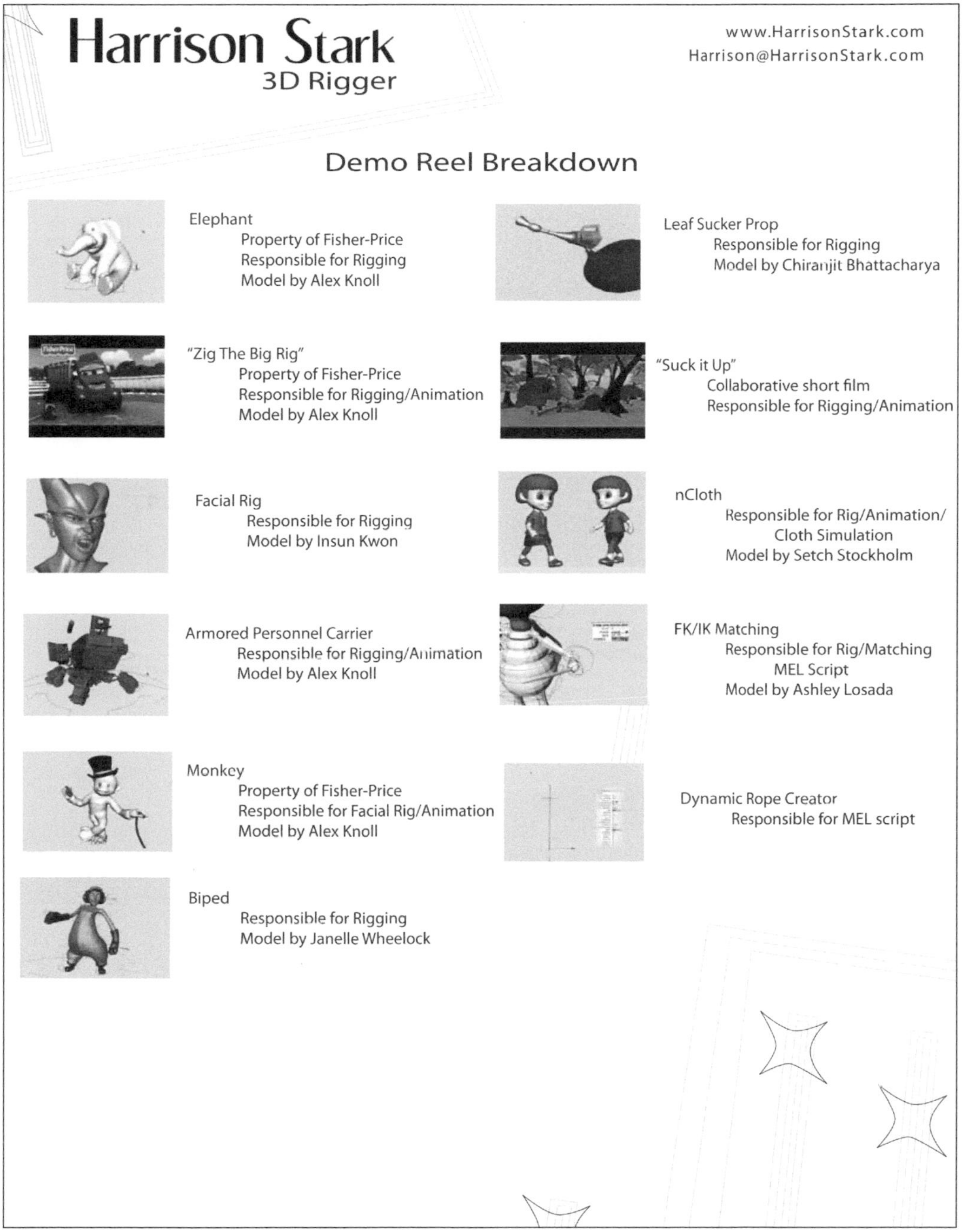

Harrison Stark
3D Rigger

www.HarrisonStark.com
Harrison@HarrisonStark.com

Demo Reel Breakdown

Elephant
Property of Fisher-Price
Responsible for Rigging
Model by Alex Knoll

Leaf Sucker Prop
Responsible for Rigging
Model by Chiranjit Bhattacharya

"Zig The Big Rig"
Property of Fisher-Price
Responsible for Rigging/Animation
Model by Alex Knoll

"Suck it Up"
Collaborative short film
Responsible for Rigging/Animation

Facial Rig
Responsible for Rigging
Model by Insun Kwon

nCloth
Responsible for Rig/Animation/
Cloth Simulation
Model by Setch Stockholm

Armored Personnel Carrier
Responsible for Rigging/Animation
Model by Alex Knoll

FK/IK Matching
Responsible for Rig/Matching
MEL Script
Model by Ashley Losada

Monkey
Property of Fisher-Price
Responsible for Facial Rig/Animation
Model by Alex Knoll

Dynamic Rope Creator
Responsible for MEL script

Biped
Responsible for Rigging
Model by Janelle Wheelock

Figure 6.6 *Example Demo Reel Breakdown by Harrison Stark. Harrison is a technical animator for Rhythm & Hues. His first job was working as a rigger for Fisher Price*

Facial Rig
Responsible for Rigging
Model by Insun Kwon

Figure 6.7 Entry From the Demo Reel Breakdown by Harrison Stark. Be careful when creating your images for your breakdown. Using .jpgs can create artifacting which makes the image look unprofessional.

Chris Jaser
CG Modeler

Chris.Jaser@gmail.com
www.ChrisJaser.com
44 Sunset Hill Road
Simsbury, CT 06070

Short Reel (30 seconds)

Shot 1: Man	Shot 2: Dragon	Shot 3: Camaro	Shot 4: P-40 Warhawk
03 seconds	10 seconds	16 seconds	21 seconds
Zbrush, Maya08	Zbrush, Maya08	Zbrush, Maya08	Zbrush, Maya08
Modeled.	Modeled and textured.	Modeled and textured.	Modeled and textured.

Long Reel (1:53 minutes)

Shot 1: Man	Shot 2: Dragon	Shot 3: Camaro	Shot 4: P-40 Warhawk
03 seconds	17 seconds	31 seconds	45 seconds
Zbrush, Maya08	Zbrush, Maya08	Zbrush, Maya08	Zbrush, Maya08
Modeled.	Modeled and textured.	Modeled and textured.	Modeled and textured.

Shot 5:Wolf	Shot 6:Piano Tree	Shot 7:Classmate	Shot 8:Sp.Ed
1 minute 7seconds	1minute 17 seconds	1minute 25 seconds	1minute 35 seconds
Zbrush, Maya08	Zbrush, Maya08	Maya08	Maya08
Modeled and textured.	Modeled and textured.	Modeled, textured, rigged, and animated for my film "SpEd"	Modeled, textured, rigged, and animated for my film "SpEd"

Sp.Ed (2:45 mintues)

Synopsis:
"Sp.Ed" is a film about a special ed. robot, who understands music rather than binary, is ridiculed by his classmates and reprimanded by his teacher. However, after finding a guitar in the trash, he finds that his disability is his greatest strength.

Medium:
Autodesk Maya
Director and creator

Figure 6.8 Example Demo Reel Breakdown by Chris Jaser. Chris is a generalist for LSI, Inc. He did an internship while still in school at Animation Collective as a production intern

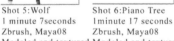

Shot 3: Camaro   Shot 4: P-40 Warhawk
31 seconds   45 seconds
Zbrush, Maya08   Zbrush, Maya08
Modeled and textured.Modeled and textured.

Figure 6.9 Entry From the Demo Reel Breakdown by Chris Jaser

In the last example of the demo reel breakdown for Becki Tower, as seen in Figure 6.10, an entire layout was created to fit inside of a DVD case. Her contact information is clearly listed at the bottom right. Numbering the thumbnails for the layout of this breakdown, with 24 pieces on her reel, would definitely have helped with the organization of the breakdown.

In a closer look at one of the items from the demo reel breakdown of Becki Tower shown in Figure 6.11, we can see the following information:

- Thumbnail of piece.
- Name of piece.
- Length of piece.
- List of software used.
- Description of what Becki did for this piece.

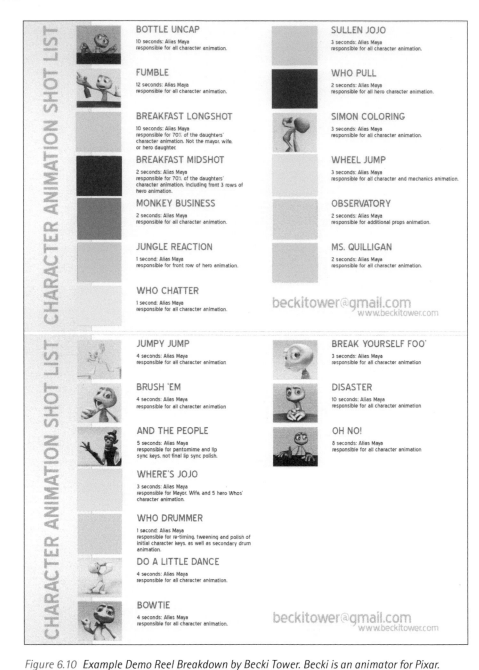

CHARACTER ANIMATION SHOT LIST

BOTTLE UNCAP
10 seconds: Alias Maya
responsible for all character animation.

FUMBLE
12 seconds: Alias Maya
responsible for all character animation.

BREAKFAST LONGSHOT
10 seconds: Alias Maya
responsible for 70% of the daughters'
character animation. Not the mayor, wife,
or hero daughter.

BREAKFAST MIDSHOT
2 seconds: Alias Maya
responsible for 70% of the daughters'
character animation, including front 3 rows of
hero animation.

MONKEY BUSINESS
2 seconds: Alias Maya
responsible for all character animation.

JUNGLE REACTION
1 second: Alias Maya
responsible for front row of hero animation.

WHO CHATTER
1 second: Alias Maya
responsible for all character animation.

SULLEN JOJO
3 seconds: Alias Maya
responsible for all character animation.

WHO PULL
2 seconds: Alias Maya
responsible for all hero character animation.

SIMON COLORING
3 seconds: Alias Maya
responsible for all character animation.

WHEEL JUMP
3 seconds: Alias Maya
responsible for all character and mechanics animation.

OBSERVATORY
2 seconds: Alias Maya
responsible for additional props animation.

MS. QUILLIGAN
2 seconds: Alias Maya
responsible for all character animation.

beckitower@gmail.com
www.beckitower.com

CHARACTER ANIMATION SHOT LIST

JUMPY JUMP
4 seconds: Alias Maya
responsible for all character animation

BRUSH 'EM
4 seconds: Alias Maya
responsible for all character animation.

AND THE PEOPLE
5 seconds: Alias Maya
responsible for pantomime and lip
sync keys, not final lip sync polish.

WHERE'S JOJO
3 seconds: Alias Maya
responsible for Mayor, Wife, and 5 hero Whos'
character animation.

WHO DRUMMER
1 second: Alias Maya
responsible for re-timing, tweening and polish of
initial character keys, as well as secondary drum
animation.

DO A LITTLE DANCE
4 seconds: Alias Maya
responsible for all character animation.

BOWTIE
4 seconds: Alias Maya
responsible for all character animation.

BREAK YOURSELF FOO'
3 seconds: Alias Maya
responsible for all character animation

DISASTER
10 seconds: Alias Maya
responsible for all character animation

OH NO!
8 seconds: Alias Maya
responsible for all character animation

beckitower@gmail.com
www.beckitower.com

Figure 6.10 Example Demo Reel Breakdown by Becki Tower. Becki is an animator for Pixar. Her first internship was as an animator at Neversoft on Guitar Hero 3. *From there she did an internship at Blue Sky Studios as an animator on* Horton Hears a Who

BRUSH 'EM

4 seconds: Alias Maya
responsible for all character animation

Figure 6.11 Entry From the Demo Reel Breakdown by Becki Tower

DO'S AND DON'TS

Be clear.

Be concise.

Make it easy to read.

Number each clip on the reel and breakdown.

Put a thumbnail image on the breakdown document of each clip.

Describe the piece briefly.

State the month and year it was created.

State if the piece is from a group project, personal project, or professional project.

Give a brief description of what you did specifically in each clip.

List what software or tools you used to make what is being shown.

Include a time log of how long the piece took to create.

Don't promote anyone but yourself.

Don't clutter the page.

Don't forget to credit others when necessary.

ACTION LIST

BRAINSTORMING

Make a list of the content of your demo reel. Include the following information:

- Number and thumbnail image.
- The month and year it was completed.
- Length of clip (time code).
- Title or description of piece.
- Was it a group project, personal project, or a professional project? If this is a professional project, what company?
- What did you do specifically?
- What software/tools did you use?
- Length of time it took for you to complete the work seen in the clip.
- Name of anyone who needs to be credited.

CREATING

- Using your letterhead, create your demo reel breakdown document.
- Rework your demo reel if necessary, adding numbers and additional text overlay or slates.

CHAPTER 7

DISTRIBUTION

DIMENSIONS AND COMPRESSION

You now have a demo reel and need to export or render the file so that you can get it distributed to as many people as possible and consequently get a job. The smallest dimensions you should export your demo reel are a resolution of 720 × 480. Of course, you want as large of a file as possible so that people can see the quality of your work. A resolution of 720p is generally adequate for this purpose, and as most people are working in HD, this is what I would recommend. However, if you have been working at a lower resolution all along, then you need to remain consistent during the export. When working on your demo reel, all the files should remain uncompressed so that you end up with the best quality. Your initial output can be uncompressed, but it is not efficient to post an uncompressed demo reel online, because the file size would be too large. No one is going to wait for an uncompressed file to download.

When outputting your demo reel, there will be settings that you need to adjust based on your area of focus. For example, if you are a Lighting Artist, you will probably be more concerned with color accuracy than an animator would. So choosing a video codec will become an area of experimentation. I recommend outputting an uncompressed version initially and then outputting different codec options for comparison. Not only are you looking at the quality of the image, you also need to look at the final file size. Ideally, you would like to end up with a file that can load quickly no matter how slow or fast the connection might be at the highest quality possible. Don't forget that you also need to consider what device or platform your demo reel will be viewed upon. Once you have an output that you like, be sure to view it on various browsers, computer platforms (both PC and Mac) as well as devices, such as smart phones and tablets.

My recommendation, if you don't have much time for experimentation, is to create an .mp4 file using the H.264 compression, which is the leading standard codec for HD quality, as shown in Figure 7.1.

If you choose to export directly as a Quicktime .mov, however, this does reduce your file size to 720 × 480, when exporting by default. You must

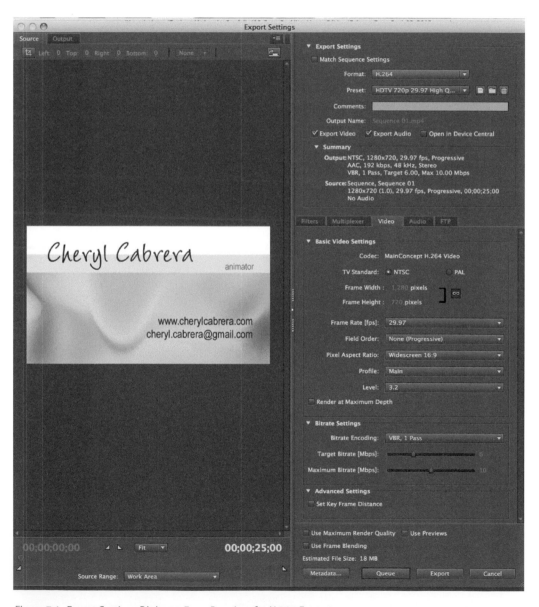

Figure 7.1 Export Settings Dialogue From Premiere for H.264 Format

change the Preset to Custom and the Width Height under Basic Settings on the Video tab to 1280 × 720, as shown in Figure 7.2.

You can also use QuickTime Player to easily export versions of your demo reel that are optimized for viewing on the internet on various connections, such as Wi-Fi, cellular, or broadband. By choosing the File > Save for Web option,

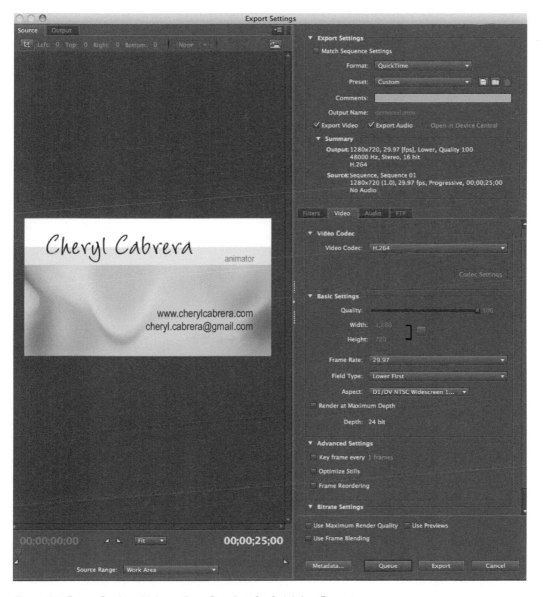

Figure 7.2 Export Settings Dialogue From Premiere for Quicktime Format

as shown in Figure 7.3 QuickTime Player will automatically create a folder that contains the movie files you need along with an HTML file that provides instructions and code that you can copy and paste into your website document. This feature uses the H.264 compression for all three versions of the movie.

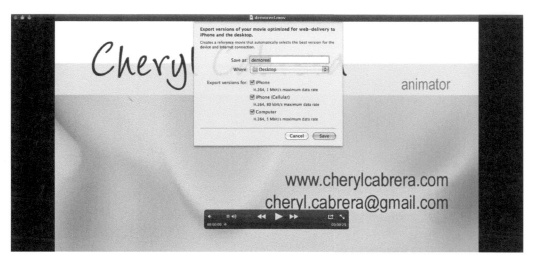

Figure 7.3 *Save for Web Options From QuickTime Player*

Be sure not to move the files that are created during the File > Save for Web process. For the code to work properly, all the files need to be in the existing folder structure, as shown in Figure 7.4.

Name	Date Modified	Size	Kind
iFrame.html	Today, 7:47 PM	4 KB	HTML ...ument
▼ Resources	Today, 7:47 PM	--	Folder
demoreel - Computer.m4v	Today, 7:47 PM	1.4 MB	protec...movie
demoreel – iPhone (Cellular).3gp	Today, 7:47 PM	115 KB	3GPP movie
demoreel – iPhone.m4v	Today, 7:47 PM	471 KB	protec...movie
demoreel.html	Today, 7:47 PM	8 KB	HTML ...ument
demoreel.jpg	Today, 7:47 PM	61 KB	JPEG image
demoreel.mov	Today, 7:47 PM	4 KB	Quick... movie
▶ images	Oct 23, 2012 4:29 PM	--	Folder
▶ scripts	Oct 23, 2012 4:29 PM	--	Folder
▶ stylesheets	Oct 23, 2012 4:29 PM	--	Folder

Figure 7.4 *The Folder Structure Created by the Save for Web Options From QuickTime Player*

Another great recommendation to follow would be those listed on the Internet Movie Database (IMDb) website. While the IMDb Demo Reel page is geared toward actors, the settings are also applicable to artists as well. The following settings are currently recommended and can be found on their website http://pro.imdb.com/help/show_leaf?prodemoreels

- **File Format:** MP4, WMV, AVI, or Quicktime
- **Codec:** H.264 / AAC, or WMV3 / AAC
- **Resolution:** 640 × 480 for SD, 1280 × 720 for HD
- **FPS:** 30 frames per second
- **Video Bitrate:** 2000 kbits/s for SD 4:3,5000 kbits/s for HD
- **Audio:** 320 kbps / 44.100 kHz
- **Deinterlacing:** On
- **Size:** Up to 500 MB
- **Length:** 10 minutes or less

WEB PUBLISHING

As discussed in Chapter 2, it is extremely important to have a web presence. The Internet is a vital tool for marketing yourself and your work. Simply having a web presence opens you to opportunities you might not have otherwise. There are many people I know who have been offered jobs to which they hadn't even applied. A recent example of this is someone I previously taught who was contacted by e-mail from Blizzard Entertainment, because they found his website and were looking to expand their World of Warcraft team. From that e-mail, he received an art test, which he passed, and as I write this, has just informed me that they have scheduled a phone interview with him.

People are always amazed when this happens, but truth be told, many companies do have recruiters who scour the Internet looking for talent. So get your work online.

WEBSITES

A portfolio website is an ideal calling card. Keep it simple, however, and make navigation easy and pain free, as shown in Figure 7.5. Create menu items that make sense. Contact information is imperative. Include an e-mail and a phone number. I know this risks being spammed, but I have had my phone number on my website for over 10 years now, and I simply don't answer unless I know who is calling me. If it is someone important, they will leave a message. So many people are afraid of being spammed that they don't put this information on the web, embed the information on their resume, or they create a form only option, but this prevents the important people from contacting you, because it creates additional investigative work to find the information. I also have an e-mail address set up specifically for my website. I use Gmail and have the e-mail from my website forwarded there, so that I don't have to remember to check a separate account. Another way to avoid being spammed, at least by bots, is to create an image .jpg or .png of your phone number and e-mail, rather than type it in your page, so that information is not searchable.

In addition to your contact information, post your demo reel, provide a downloadable file as well as a streamable one, a link to your breakdown, and additional portfolio pieces. You can use your breakdown as a webpage and make the thumbnails link to individual clips. Take some time to develop a page that shows your process for each piece. Just keep the organization simple and clear. You don't want to frustrate the visitor by making navigation so complicated that they can't find anything.

The purpose of the website, as well as your demo reel, is to showcase your best work. You can also post information about works-in-progress and reveal part of your thought process by showcasing the evolution of a piece. A blog can be used for this purpose, because it is easier to update regularly than a website.

Using basic HTML instead of more complicated web plugins allows your work to be searchable and device friendly. Test your website on various devices, browsers, and operating systems to ensure that everything displays properly.

DVDs

Only a few short years ago, DVDs were considered the medium used as industry standard for demo reel submission. Not so anymore. Most studios want to simply go online and view your reel on the web. Vimeo is a popular place for posting your reel. If you decide to burn DVDs or in a rare case one is asked for submissions, make sure to test the reel on multiple devices and make sure that it plays on an actual DVD player, not just on the computer. If they can't look at your reel because of technical problems, you pretty much have blown your chance at getting an interview. Make sure you test it on as many different DVD players and computers as you can; one at home,

Figure 7.5 Sample Website Homepage of Aaron Morse. Notice the Clear Navigation

at school, ask a friend, ask your neighbor, PC, and MAC. I must also include here that DVD-r seems to be the most compatible with the most devices.

One of my former students, Tonya Payne (who also acted as the editor for this book), actually got her first job using a DVD. She had applied through their website before graduation, but never heard anything from that submission, so she sent her materials through snail mail. The Producer had them call her, because her physical demo reel on DVD landed on his desk. Apparently they did not get many submissions like that anymore.

GETTING YOUR REEL CRITIQUED

WEB COMMUNITIES

Chapter 4 talked about online forums as a place for networking. Becoming involved in online communities is a great way for networking and feedback opportunities. They also provide you with opportunities to help others.

But online forums and web communities also provide a place to get your demo reel and portfolio critiqued. One of my former students, as he was approaching graduation, posted his demo reel on cgsociety.org and asked for some feedback. Not only did he get some good suggestions for improvement, he was also contacted and offered jobs at three different studios.

Some of the most commonly used online forums are the following:

forums.cgsociety.org/

www.cgchannel.com/

forums.awn.com/

www.creativecrash.com/forums

conceptart.org

forums.3dtotal.com/

www.vfxtalk.com

area.autodesk.com/forum

http://www.sidefx.com/forum

You can also pay for your demo reel to be critiqued:

http://www.reelfeedback.com/free-reel-review/

http://www.rateareel.com/index.cfm

GETTING YOUR DEMO REEL INTO THE RIGHT HANDS

Once you have a reel, in addition to applying for jobs through company websites and job boards, you can also distribute your reel to people who may have an inside to other job opportunities that may not be advertised. I have known many who have been offered job opportunities, because they knew someone through contacts they had made who are members of a union or guild, through attendance at trade association conferences or trade shows, or by participation in film festivals or contests.

UNIONS AND GUILDS

A union is an organized group of workers who collectively use their strength to have a voice in their workplace. A guild is a union made up of artisans. Some of the benefits of membership in a union include free legal advice, better health benefits, paid overtime, job listings, and job referrals.

Some states are "Forced-Unionism" states, which means if a company that has a collective bargaining agreement on file with a union employs you, then you must join the union and pay dues. Other states are considered "Right to Work" states, which gives employees the right to decide whether or not they want to join a union. Once a studio under union contract hires you, you are sent an informational packet and asked to join.

The International Alliance of Theatrical Stage Employees, Moving Picture Technicians, Artists, and Allied Crafts of the United States, its Territories and Canada (IATSE) is the largest union representing workers in the entertainment industry. Unfortunately, while IATSE touts the word "International" in its name, its jurisdiction covers only the United States, its Territories, and Canada. Unions are not allowed in many countries, and in some countries, a person can even get killed if they join one. Until this changes, or something else does, the unions have little leverage in preventing outsourcing work from the United States to other countries.

IATSE is the parent organization of the Animation Guild, Local 839, which covers Animators, Background Matte Painters, Character Designers, Layout Artists, CG Modelers, Riggers, Storyboard Artists, and Scriptwriters for animation. The Animation Guild has or has had in the past collective bargaining agreements with the following studios:

Dreamworks Animation SKG

Disney Feature Animation

Sony Pictures Animation

Imagemovers Digital

Nickelodeon

Screen Actors Guild and the American Federation of Television and Radio Artists (SAG-AFTRA) covers the voice talent and actors, as well as other types of performers.

Other guilds that may be of some interest to you are:

American Federation of Musicians (AFM)

International Cinematographers Guild (ICG)

Motion Picture Editors Guild (MPEG)

The latest contracted wage minimums, medians, and maximums can be found here:

http://animationguild.org/contracts-wages/

Both IATSE and SAG-AFTRA fall under the umbrella organization of the American Federation of Labor and Congress of Industrial Organizations (AFL-CIO).

TRADE ASSOCIATIONS

A trade association, also known as an industry trade group, is organized, founded, and funded by the businesses of a particular industry. The main focus is collaboration between companies in the association. Joining one of these associations provide wonderful opportunities because many of them hold professional conferences, additional networking opportunities, and offer workshops and classes. Most of the associations are nonprofit. Attendance and participation at an annual trade show or conference opens doors for many opportunities for networking and exposure.

The following are some associations that I have personal experience with, but there are many more. Please check out the website www.reelsuccess.com for links to these and others. You can usually join one of these associations by signing up on their website and paying annual dues.

www.siggraph.org: Association for Computing Machinery—Special Interest Group on Computer Graphics and Interactive Techniques (ACM-SIGGRAPH) is a community of people interested in computer graphics and interactive techniques. Figure 7.6 shows the exhibition floor from the SIGGRAPH 2009 conference in New Orleans.

Figure 7.6 Exhibition Floor at the Annual SIGGRAPH Conference

www.asifa.net: Association Internationale du Film D' Animation (ASIFA) with over 5,000 members in 55 countries is dedicated to the animated film as an art and communication form.

www.igda.org: The International Game Developers Association (IGDA) is the largest nonprofit membership organization in the world serving all individuals who create video games.

www.promaxbda.org: Promax BDA (Broadcast Designers Association) is a nonprofit, full-service, membership-driven association for promotion and marketing professionals working in broadcast media.

www.womeninanimation.org: Women In Animation (WIA) is a professional, nonprofit organization established to foster the dignity, concerns, and advancement of women who are involved in any and all aspects of the art and industry of animation.

> To avoid criticism say nothing, do nothing, be nothing.
>
> Aristotle

FILM AND ANIMATION FESTIVALS

Completing, submitting, and being accepted into animation or film festivals gives you an opportunity to publicize your website at the end of your film and, in turn, open the door for potential employers or recruiters to contact you. The biggest part of this equation is actually completing a film. I have been both a juror and an attendee for several animation and film festivals, and I am always amazed at what actually gets into them. The message here is to complete a film and submit it. We are always our own worst critic, and you just never know what a jury is looking for or what other submissions have been entered that year.

There are many festivals that have no entry fees. Just be aware that because of this, the competition is much more fierce than those that do require a fee. This part of the process can become a pricey expenditure, especially when there is no guarantee for acceptance.

The biggest resource for film festival entry submissions is www.withoutabox .com. On this website, you can create a project file for each of your films that simplifies the submission process. You can upload trailers, clips, posters, and photos. You can create a press-kit and actually submit your film digitally using a secure online screener to 850 different festivals. You can do an advanced search of over 5,000 festivals worldwide to meet the criteria of your film. There is actually a dropdown list of all the festivals that are animation festivals, IMDb qualifiers (just submitting to one of these gives you an IMDb page), and Oscar boosters (where winning one of these festivals puts you into step for qualifying for the Academy Awards). Using Withoutabox is free.

Be aware that Withoutabox does not currently have every single festival available. Other festivals can be found simply by searching online for local, national, or international festivals.

COMPETITIONS AND CONTESTS

There are always different contests or competitions where you can both develop work that can be put onto your reel, and you might also actually win some money or other opportunity. Working toward a deadline gives you experience working under pressure. So if you are not in school, it is good to keep improving your skills and developing new work.

Some of these competitions or contests are part of a film festival or conference; others are online opportunities, whereas others have corporate sponsors. The additional benefit of exposure is also a perk. Do some research because some of these competitions are a one-time opportunity, whereas others repeat monthly or annually. Always keep your eyes open for new opportunities.

My former students have won some of the following competitions in previous years: Big cash prizes and some nice opportunities to meet with studio executives. They have gone on to do amazing work for companies like ILM, Sony Feature Animation, and Disney Feature Animation.

Japan Media Arts Festival, j-mediaarts.jp

Crackle.com's Wet Paint competition, www.crackle.com/

KAFI's Cartoon Challenge, www.kafi.kvcc.edu (this festival no longer exists at this time)

Doritos Krash the Superbowl Challenge

11 second club, http://www.11secondclub.com/

Animate it! http://www.animate-it.com/category/competition/

The following sites have competition postings:

Aniboom, http://www.aniboom.com/competition/all

Graphic Competitions, http://www.graphiccompetitions.com/animation/

Dexigner, http://www.dexigner.com/design-competitions/Animation

DO's AND DON'Ts

Export your demo reel using the best quality and size for the device, HD if at all possible.

Keep your file size small using H.264 compression for HD.

Adjust the Gamma if necessary.

Take time to experiment with output settings to get the best look.

Use Quicktime .mov files

Keep originals uncompressed.

Export an uncompressed version to have available.

Create a website.

Keep website navigation simple.

Be sure your contact information is easily found on your website.

Stick with HTML so that you can be searchable and visible on multiple devices.

Don't forget to test your website on different devices, browsers, and operating systems.

Post your demo reel for download and also make it streamable.

Join web communities, give feedback, and get feedback on your reel.

Join a Trade Association. Attend a conference.

Create an animated short film and enter it into festivals.

Find a contest or competition and enter!

Don't stop creating new work.

ACTION LIST

BRAINSTORMING

- Research online communities that share your area of interest.
- Search and create a list of Trade Associations that share your interests.
- Search for contests and competitions that you can work toward for new demo reel pieces.
- Begin conception of a short film that you can work toward for new demo reel pieces.

CREATING

- Export your reel.
- Create your website if you have not done so already.
- Post your demo reel online.
- Post your demo reel on web communities and ask for feedback.

CHAPTER 8

THE INTERVIEW

So you have applied to a studio or a job posting. What can you expect after you have submitted your materials? Well, if the position is still open and you have met the qualifications, you will be contacted through either e-mail or phone to let you know that they are interested in you as a candidate. This process can take less than 1 day, a few weeks, or even several years. One of my former students just posted on Facebook that a company contacted him in January 2012 for a position that he applied for in May 2009. I asked him if the company had given him a heads up or a letter saying that they liked his work and they would keep it on file, and his response was no, he hadn't heard anything from them until January 2012.

How could this be, you might ask? If a studio thinks your work is good but not a fit for the current position (or the position is already filled), they may shelve your resume and portfolio and return to it when another position opens where you are a fit.

WHEN SHOULD I FOLLOW UP?

If you haven't heard back from a company after the initial application, there could be several reasons. Maybe they did not receive your materials. Perhaps they are not interested. Or maybe they're just really too busy and they haven't had a chance to look at your application materials yet. Or maybe they've already hired somebody. You can follow up probably after 2 weeks of applying if you haven't heard anything through e-mail or phone, but don't be surprised if you don't receive a response to your follow-up. It really depends on how busy they are. I really don't think they're trying to be rude. Don't annoy them with follow-up phone calls or e-mails either. If, after 3 months, you still haven't heard anything and you're still interested in working for that company, I would recommend that you submit a new demo reel with mostly new work on it, at least half of the reel or more. Don't ever send in the same demo reel. Ever. You're just wasting your time and theirs. And time is money.

HOW TO PREPARE

Check your local university or business career center and see if they will schedule a mock interview for practice. The more prepared you are, the more relaxed you will be when the time comes.

When you are contacted, you want to be able to present yourself as a team player so that they can see how you fit in with the other members of the studio. To show that you are capable of doing what you represent on your demo reel, you must be willing to do anything that they want you to do.

Be prepared to give three references, if you haven't been asked already. Make sure that these references are willing to give you a really great recommendation. Ask them. I have been asked to give recommendations many, many, many times. I say yes even if it is a bad one. It is up to you to clarify with the person you are asking whether the recommendation will be a good one. If someone asks me to clarify, I will tell him or her yes, if I can, or no, if I cannot give a good one.

You want to be able to communicate to them how you can help them and that you will be an asset to their team. You want to show your enthusiasm and that you're willing to learn and do whatever it takes to get the job done. You want to show them that you are a good problem solver.

Do your research. If your interview is with a movie company try to watch every movie that they've done in the last 5–10 years. If it's a gaming company, make sure you've played their last 3–5 titles. One of the worst things you can do in an interview is go in and tell them that you've never played their games or watched their movies or that you don't like to play games or watch movies. They will wonder why you want to work at their studio, or in this industry altogether. Learn everything you can about the studio and the city where it is located. It is important to research cost of living in the area where the studio is located and have a good idea for salary expectations. This information can be sometimes difficult to find. Utilize your networking contacts to see if anyone can help you find a realistic number.

For each company you apply to, create a "cheat sheet" of notes to have on hand for the phone interview or for reviewing prior to an in-person interview, as in Figure 8.1.

Studio Name:
Application sent: month/day/year

Follow-up:

How I heard about the job:
Personal contacts at this company:

Job Description:

Notable Projects:

Location:
Information about area and cost of living:

Figure 8.1 Sample "Cheat Sheet" Format

Once you are contacted, you will either be scheduled initially for an art test or a phone interview.

THE ART TEST

Most gaming companies, and some film studios, are apt to give an art test if they are interested in you as a potential employee. The purpose of the art test is to see what you can do under a constrained time frame with a deadline. You will probably be asked to sign an NDA (nondisclosure agreement). An NDA is a document that basically states that you cannot discuss anything with anyone who works outside of the studio. Be sure to ask questions to clarify any aspects of the art test that may be confusing. Please take all the allotted time that is given to you to complete the test.

Art tests are directly related to the position to which you are applying. Sometimes studios provide asset files for you to use during your art test. Some sample art tests that I, or someone I know, have been given are:

1. Animate a run, walk, jump, and death sequence. (A character rig is given, and usually a frame length such as 12 frame run).
2. Model, UV, and texture (a particular character, prop, or environment).
3. Here is a character rig. Re rig the character and animate a walk cycle.

The time frame given for an art test is usually 72 hours to 2 weeks.

Be cautious when asked to do an art test. If the company is established and reputable, everything should be fine. I have, however, heard of some start-up companies using art tests as a way of getting free work completed, with no real intention of hiring anyone. If you were asked to do an art test by a company without a decent history, I would get in writing that they are not allowed to use your work without proper compensation.

THE PHONE INTERVIEW

During the phone interview, one or more people will formally question you. Treat the phone interview just as you would be an interview that is in-person. I believe people do phone interviews for two reasons. First, it allows them to screen candidates without the cost of an in-person experience. Second, it allows the candidates to focus on the conversation, rather than appearance.

Try not to say the words uh, um, and like. This is a hard habit to break, but one worth the concentration and energy. Don't be too long winded when answering questions. Be conscientious of your grammar. Don't use slang or swear. Be aware of the speed of your words when you speak because you don't want to be too fast or too slow. Be mindful of your volume; don't be too loud or too low.

Be careful that you do not come across as arrogant, overconfident, aggressive, egotistical, insecure, unfriendly, ditzy, absentminded, or desperate.

QUESTIONS AND ANSWERS

There are endless possibilities for questions and answers during both the phone interview and in-person interview. The main impression you want to make when answering the questions is that you are truly inspired by the work that their studio creates, confident in your abilities, and interested in working at their studio. You should project a positive attitude, but do not come across as "kissing up" or "brown-nosing" them. Be sincere, not fake.

Be on the lookout for trick questions and don't speak negatively about a previous position, coworker, or boss. Suppose you are asked about a current project that you are working on which is under a nondisclosure agreement, and it is hinted that it is safe to show that work in the interview. Your current interviewer is probably trying to test your integrity and honor. If you talk badly about your previous position, coworker, or boss during your interview, it is highly likely that this is something you would repeat, not to mention the fact that this industry is small and they are likely to know the person you are talking about.

This question is always asked:

> Why do you want to work here?

A good answer could be something like this:

> I've always been a fan of your studio's work, and it would be an honor to be part of such an amazingly creative team.

Be prepared for follow-up questions such as:

> Well then, what specifically do you like about our projects?

Always relate your answers to the creative aspects of your work, not to practical reasons. Answers such as the following should be avoided, even if they are true:

> I've always wanted to live in Los Angeles.

> I really need a job to pay off my student loans, and this is the best I can find.

THE IN-PERSON INTERVIEW

WHAT TO WEAR

> Nothing you wear is more important than your smile
>
> Connie Stevens

In addition to the tips above for the phone interview, an in-person interview necessitates additional advice. When you arrive at an in-person interview, you want to make a great first impression. As shallow as it might seem, we, as human beings, really do judge people by how they present themselves physically. Make sure to take time with personal grooming and choose appropriate attire so that you can make a strong visual first impression.

Your physical appearance should be clean and well groomed. Take a shower, shave, and get a haircut. Don't wear too much perfume. You will be in close quarters with several people and probably nervous. Be aware of your personal odor. Stay away from foods that are known to create body odor: spicy foods, alcohol, red meat, dairy products, onions, and garlic. Stay away from tobacco, as well.

Don't overdress for the interview. This industry does not expect you to wear a suit and tie, or a dress to the interview. Business casual attire is appropriate here. In fact, a nice pair of jeans and button up shirt is not unusual, but be careful not to underdress. Go with your personality and the personality of the studio. Take care not to look messy or outdated. Take time to iron your clothes. Nothing you wear should be too tight, flashy, or revealing.

Practice good body language. Make comfortable eye contact with people when you speak to them. When you shake their hand, be firm but not too forceful. You should never squeeze someone's hand stronger than the grip they have on yours. Be careful not to fidget or giggle nervously. Be mindful of how you act. You want to come across as sincere and self-confident, not awkward. Most importantly, don't forget to smile.

WHAT TO BRING

Coming prepared to a job interview shows your potential employer that you respect their time and that you pay attention to detail. There are several items that you should absolutely bring to a job interview:

- A copy of your reel and a device on which to play it.
- A flatbook portfolio of drawings or other 2D work that is not on your reel.
- A clean copy of your resume and cover letter. Bring enough copies for each interviewer. If you are unsure, bring 10.
- Any new work that you may have and want to show.
- Five to ten questions prepared to ask your interviewers.
- Your "cheat sheet" of information related to this job application.
- Anything else that you have been asked to bring.

You may also want to have the following with you:

- A pen and small notebook.
- Inside the notebook, have the following:
  - The name, title, and phone number of the person you are meeting.
  - The names of the people from the phone interview.
  - A copy of the job posting or job description.
  - Any additional agenda notes, directions to the studio (if you are driving there).
  - An extra copy of your resume for you to refer to if necessary.
  - A list of references and work history with names, addresses, phone numbers, and dates of employment.
  - The five to ten questions that you have prepared to ask your interviewers.
- Your cell phone (turned off or muted).
- A small snack, such as a protein bar. (They will most likely take you to lunch, but it doesn't hurt to have something with you if needed.)
- Breath mints.

Be punctual! Arrive on time or about 5 minutes early.

WHEN WILL I HEAR A DECISION?

Immediately following the phone interview or the in-person interview, you should send out thank you notes as discussed in Chapter 2. An e-mail thank you after the phone interview is sufficient. A handwritten thank you note

> In a job interview, you may be up against nine competitors. Be ready to state your focus more clearly than your nine rivals. Know your focus or get beaten by the competition who knows theirs.
>
> Alan Fox

> If you're going on even an entry-level job interview, take the time to follow up with a handwritten note, even if your handwriting isn't the best and even if you can't use four-syllable words. Just showing that initiative makes a difference. If someone takes the time to write a note ... I've had many employers tell me it's a way they make a decision about hiring.
>
> Cindy Zimmermann

> Our greatest weakness lies in giving up. The most certain way to succeed is always to try just one more time.
>
> Thomas A. Edison

after an in-person interview is best. After the art test or a phone interview, it can take anywhere from a week to several months to hear anything. For an in-person interview, you should hear a decision within a couple of weeks. It really does depend on how many other candidates are being interviewed for the same position. It is perfectly fine at the end of your interview to ask when you should expect to hear something.

If you are not hired, you can always reapply. Make sure to wait approximately 6 months before you resubmit your materials and make sure that you have added or changed at least 30% of your reel. There are always new opportunities developing.

NEGOTIATING A CONTRACT

Once the studio decides to hire you, you will usually be offered an employment contract, as in Figure 8.2. The time to negotiate your contract begins before the offer is made. During your interview process, you will usually meet with someone in HR, if it is a larger company. That is the time to ask about benefits, such as relocation assistance, medical and dental benefits, retirement options, stock options, as well as noncompete and nondisclosure agreements. At no time should you bring up salary. Wait for them to broach the subject.

It is important to have a good idea of what you are expecting in the salary range. Because you did stellar research earlier about the company, cost of living, and salary median for your job, you should already know what pay range should be offered to you. Be aware that salaries fluctuate depending on location of the studio.

Some companies have a flat pay rate, such as $40,000 annual USD for all new hires. This amount doesn't seem like much, especially for the cost of living in the Los Angeles area. Be sure to ask about overtime compensation. This amount is definitely not acceptable if there is no overtime. I know people, however, who with overtime have ended up making well over $100,000 a year with a base salary of $40,000.

If an employer asks you what salary you expect, be sure to give them a range but understand that they will probably go with the lower end of that range. Realize that if they are offering you a contract, then they truly are interested in hiring you. Don't be afraid to ask for what you deserve, just make sure it is based on realistic existing figures. The worst that can happen is that they say "No." Just counter with, "Well, ok then, what did you have in mind?"

Dear Cheryl:

I am pleased to offer you the position of Designer for Company X. In this position, you will be reporting to Jim Smith, CEO. You will be starting your employment with Company X on June 1, 2013 in our New York office located at 123 First Street, New York NY.

Your Base Salary will be at the rate of $65,000 on an annualized basis.

In addition, you will be eligible to receive a bonus of $10,000 which will be paid on your first anniversary. Additionally, there will be a discretionary bonus based on company financial results ranging between $1,000 -$10,000. The company will need to meet certain criteria and objectives.

In addition to your Base Salary, you will be eligible to participate in the Company X benefit programs as set forth in the Benefits Booklet and schedule. Please note that all benefits are subject to change at the Company's sole discretion. You will be eligible for 1 week vacation after 6 months employment, 2 weeks after one year of employment, and 3 weeks after three years employment.

In order to commence your employment with Company X, it will be necessary for you to submit several forms and documents, including an Application for Employment, an I-9 Form, and a Non-Disclosure/Non-Competition Agreement (attached). In order to complete the I-9 Form, you must bring valid proof of your identity and your authorization to work in the United States on your first day of employment. Please refer to the attachment for appropriate documentation.

This offer is conditioned upon your successful completion of a background check, including verification by a third party, of prior employment history, education and record of convictions. Please be aware that false statements, failure to disclose information, or failure to submit required documents may disqualify you from employment or, if employed, result in your immediate dismissal.

This offer is also contingent upon your agreement to the terms of the enclosed Non-Disclosure/Non-Competition Agreement, as well as on your representation that you have disclosed to the Company any obligations or duties owed to previous employers, or other persons or entities that would prohibit, or conflict with, performing your duties and obligations to the Company.

Please understand that your employment with Company X is "at will" meaning that you may terminate your employment with Company X at any time and for any reason whatsoever simply by notifying the Company. Likewise, Company X may terminate your employment at any time and for any reason, with or without cause or advance notice. Please also understand that your acceptance of this offer should not be based on any promises or representations other than those contained in this letter. Any promises contrary to the terms specified in this letter are superseded by this offer letter.

Please acknowledge your acceptance of this offer by returning a copy of (i) this offer letter and (ii) the enclosed Non-Disclosure/Non-Competition Agreement, each properly executed by you, within ten days of the date of this letter. If not received within 10 days, the offer will be deemed withdrawn.

We are very excited about you joining us at Company X.

Sincerely,

Acknowledged and agreed to: _____
Date: _____

Enclosures

Figure 8.2 Example Employment Contract

> Most of the important things in the world have been accomplished by people who have kept on trying when there seemed to be no hope at all.
>
> Dale Carnegie

FREELANCING

There may be a time where you find yourself in a position to do freelance work. Perhaps you have been approached by a friend of the family or maybe you can't seem to find full-time employment, so you are looking to supplement your income or simply get experience by working on smaller projects to add to your reel. Many people don't have any idea where to start, and I am frequently asked, "How much should I charge for a freelance project?"

First, I must establish the fact that you must have legal software to create work and get paid. If you don't have a budget to pay for professional software licenses, there are freeware alternatives available that can be used.

www.gimp.org/

www.gimpshop.com/

www.blender.org

If working on a long-term contract as a freelancer for a company, you should be provided with a software license for any software that is needed. The license can be relinquished when you stop working for them.[1]

If you are working in the United States, the costs for software licenses can be written off on your taxes. You're going to need a good and honest certified public accountant (CPA) if you do 1099 freelance. You should put aside 15%–25% of your pay for taxes (an additional 10%–20% if you have State income tax), and you must make quarterly payments after the first year of freelance income. Definitely seek tax advice, or you can wind up in trouble with the IRS. When you have few expenses to write off, you can wind up with a huge tax bill on April 15.[2] So be very careful.

Second, finding freelance opportunities can be achieved by registering at any or all the following websites, where you can post your portfolio and bid on prospective projects.

www.odesk.com

www.guru.com

www.aniboom.com

www.freelancer.com

www.elance.com

The best approach to freelance is to have an established rate per project as well as an established hourly rate that can be charged when necessary. For example, a minute of animation may run between US$1,000 and US$1,500 and take 2 weeks to complete. This can include one or two client review sessions and provide them an opportunity for feedback at pivotal points of the project. Additional sessions can be an option for an additional charge.

You basically want to create a menu of services that you are willing to offer, along with prices and estimated time frames for those services. The client is then aware of the costs; especially the cost for changes that they make after the agreement has been made. Protect yourself by creating a contract that specifies exactly what is expected, when it will be delivered, and any charges for additional changes. If you are asked to sign a contract, you should have a lawyer read it. You should also have a lawyer read any contract that you draw up, unless you are using one that has already been vetted by someone with legal knowledge.

If you have been documenting how long it takes for you to complete aspects of your projects, creating this menu of services should be an easy task. If you haven't done this, you will need to begin with an estimate and make adjustments as you go along.

An hourly rate can be anywhere from US$12 to US$100. It can vary based on the type of service offered. Just be careful not to undersell yourself or anyone else in the business. Again, do some research as to how much is an acceptable current rate. The Animation Guild website is a great place to start. *The Graphic Artist's Guild Handbook of Pricing and Ethical Guidelines* is also a valuable resource.

> Twenty years from now you will be more disappointed by the things you didn't do than by the ones you did do. So throw off the bowlines. Sail away from the safe harbor. Catch the trade winds in your sails. Explore. Dream. Discover.
>
> Mark Twain

DO's AND DON'Ts

Two weeks after submitting your materials, follow up with a company to ensure receipt.

Don't annoy anyone with repeated inquiries.

Continue to create new work for your reel.

Wait for 3–6 months before reapplying to the same company.

Don't resubmit the same materials.

Be prepared to give three good references.

Research the companies that you have applied to and learn as much as you can about the work that they do.

Research the cities where these studios are located.

Know how much the current salary is for your specialty area.

Practice interviewing with friends or sign up for a mock interview.

Practice not saying words like uh, um, and like.

Practice not using slang or swear words.

Practice speaking at a moderate pace.

Be mindful of your volume when speaking.

Have an outfit ready for interviews. Keep at least two or three options available, in case of multiple day interviews.

Send thank you e-mails immediately following your phone interview.

Send thank you letters immediately following your in-person interview.

Explore options for freelance opportunities.

ACTION LIST

BRAINSTORMING

- Research the companies that you have applied to and learn as much as you can about the work that they do.
- Research the cities where these studios are located.
- Research what the current salary is for your specialty area.
- Put together two or three interview ready outfits.
- If interested in freelancing, begin thinking about what areas you would like to offer creative services.

CREATING

- Create a "cheat sheet" for each job you apply to which contains the following information:
  - The company or studio name.
  - The date your application was sent.

- Leave space to make notations, dates, and times of follow-up e-mails or phone calls.
- The job description.
- Names of anyone that you know at that company.
- Specific projects that the studio has created with brief descriptive notes and your thoughts on each project.
- Information about the location and cost of living.
- Create your freelancer's menu that states the following:
  - List of services offered with prices and time frame needed.
  - Hourly rates for various services.
- Create a rough draft of your freelance contract.
- Register on freelance websites.

NOTES

1   This information is direct input from my editor, Tonya Payne.
2   Ibid.

APPENDIX

AN INTERVIEW WITH JOEY LENZ

At the time of this interview, Joey Lenz was a graduate student in the
Visual Effects department at the Savannah College of Art and Design (SCAD).
I interviewed Joey, because I did not have him as a student. Joey asked to
friend me on Facebook, because we shared several friends (utilizing his
networking skills). From there, I noticed some of the work that he posted, and
a status that said he had an interview with Dreamworks. I then contacted
him for an interview. The demo reel he used to get this interview with
Dreamworks is posted on www.reelsuccess.com. He has since obtained an
internship that begins June 2013 with Microsoft Game Studios. You can
check out his current work on his website at http://polyplant.co/.

Figure A.1 Website of Joey Lenz: Polyplant.co

Question: How did you go about getting your interview and what did you do to prepare for that interview?

Answer: Well I think one of the most important things for an interview, in my opinion, especially something that I had to do at this school, is put together a professional presentation. I know some of my friends have tried getting an interview before they had a nice complete package, and they didn't get one. More particularly you have to have something that sticks out about yourself; focus on a particular area of 3D: whether it's lighting, animation, or something else. If you have too much of a generalist reel (which I did for a little while and I'm working on tuning that up), they told me that I need to focus on a particular area and have nothing else. I think when you talk to people who are at different companies you've got to be really passionate about what you're interested in, because if you can't sell yourself to them, be able to talk to them and sound like you're passionate, they probably will not want to work with you. At these studios you're working long hours, and they want to be able to work with someone that they can tolerate and want to be around. That's another thing I've noticed.

As far as the reel in particular, I think (depending on what you are focusing on) you should not be scared to show reference material. For example, if you borrowed concept art from somewhere, show where you got your reference, your inspiration. I would also say if you did a team project (which they always look for—they want you to show that you can work collaboratively with others) show what responsibilities you were in charge of during the demo reel. For the resume, let them know if you've done stuff other than just 3D, something interesting that makes you stick out, those are always good things. I believe you need to include this information in your resume because it says that you're a unique person, and that you can do more than just work with the computer.

Question: So you're talking about in a field unrelated to 3D or in art in general?

Answer: For instance, I used to be a volunteer firefighter for 2 years, and that in itself has some skills that can translate over to the 3D studio environment. It shows that I can work with others, that I know how to be a team player, and it shows that I can work under pressure. You can bring a lot of different skills and experiences from other areas and include that in what you do as an artist.

Question: How did you get the interview? What was the process in doing that?

Answer: What these studios want is that you have a website available, especially these days. It used to be you had to have a Flatbook and things of more of a physical manner. Now they are more and more interested in digital portfolios where everything is paperless. If you're going to something like a career fair or get an interview through your school when a company visits, you need to have a business card, a resume, and breakdown sheets. These are important because they want to know exactly what you did and what you were responsible for. Also bring a DVD. It's good to have a label on the DVD so that it doesn't look like you just slapped it together.

Question: So you're saying the more professional you look the better?

Answer: I always feel presentation is a big deal because half of the battle is having really good work. The other half is who you are, your presentation, and how you present all of your work.

Question: Did you apply through the studio website? Or was it through the school?

Answer: The interviews that I have had thus far have been through the school, but I have also been applying to a lot of different websites. It's a combination of a lot of different things. Another great source is having friends either through Facebook or actually in real life (not from networking around). They've given me inside contacts and I've talked to some of the other studios that way, too. There are many ways that I do it.

Question: So tell me what feedback you got from Dreamworks, specifically last week when you interviewed with them.

Answer: The biggest thing they said about my body of work was that it was a little too generalized.

Question: So did they give you some suggestions for what you should do to improve?

Answer: Yes, they said I need to really focus on one area or another, depending on my interest. But they said it's not like I have to start all over. I can take what I already have and reorganize it and how it's perceived. Also, I need to include specific types of work. For example, I have this one big project at the beginning of my reel that shows I did modeling, lighting, compositing and all that. They wanted to know more specifically what am I interested in doing. These studios don't operate with generalists usually. They want people who are specialized and fit within a certain part of the pipeline. So it all depends on how it's perceived. If I have a big project that is like a generalist piece, maybe at the beginning of my reel I can have a live action integration piece or something that shows lighting specifically, and then my reel can be taken more in a lighting manner, you know, how it's perceived. So that's the biggest suggestion they gave me.

Question: Great, so what area do you think is your main focus, or will be?

Answer: My main area of focus and interest right now will be lighting. I also think it is really important that you have a backup plan in case your main thing doesn't go through, and so my backup I'm going to be focusing on is hard surface modeling.

Question: Have you done an art test for any of the places that you have interviewed?

Answer: Yes, Sony PlayStation up in Santa Monica. I had to do an art test for them because they wanted proof of ability. I notice a lot of game studios are like that. I haven't noticed that as much with Visual Effects Studios.

Question: So can you talk about that art test a little bit, about what they asked you to do and what time frame did they give you?

Answer: I can't go into the details specifically of what the art test was about because I was under an NDA, but I was basically given as much time as I wanted to which was a little unusual for me. One of the reasons why I think I didn't succeed at it was because I didn't have prior game experience or knowledge and understanding of gaming techniques at the time, so I was trying to figure it all out as I was doing the art test. And more importantly, I don't play video games, so when I made this asset for this art test I underdelivered. Say they wanted something 50,000 polygons I did it in 5,000, I thought maybe, "Oh, I'm showing I'm really efficient. This is for a video game. You know it can handle only so much, so I want to show that I can be really efficient." Well that's not the case. PSD is actually a lot more powerful than I estimated it to be. So whenever these studios want specifically a certain amount of polygons or texture resolutions deliver at that amount. And if you're not for sure, ask questions. That's another big thing. I didn't ask enough questions.

Question: Would they allow you to ask those questions to get clear on what they wanted?

Answer: Yes, Mmmm Hmmm.

Question: When you did go into the interview with Dreamworks, what did you bring with you? Did you bring the actual demo reel with you again?

Answer: Beyond just turning in my package into SCAD, where they hand it off to Dreamworks, I usually bring in my smart phone because I can play video on it. It's an extra copy of the reel in case something doesn't play. It's good to have a back up. Then also I bring in my flash drive because I have additional work that's not on my reel and I can show them if they are more interested in seeing that. Even work that is on my reel, but I went back and retouched up some of those projects but didn't have the resources and time to touch up my reel. So I bring a couple of stills of what it would look like if I had the resources and time to achieve that.

Question: When you are putting together your demo reel, were you given any guidelines as far as what media to put it on? Did you have to provide it on DVD format? If not, on the web, is there a specific codec or platform that you have it so that you can play it?

Answer: I was recommended that no more than 2 minutes. You want enough to show them that you have some good content but you want to leave enough to where they want to see more. As far as a specific medium, if you're doing it by a physical means, a DVD. I prefer to have it on the web. On my website I'm using Vimeo. So I have everything embedded on my website from Vimeo. The specific codec I use is H264. It keeps the files pretty small and manageable. I have to do a little color correction to it, because H264 gives you this really bright, desaturated look. It's just how Quicktime reads it.

Question: What was the length of your reel that you showed them?

Answer: My reel was around 1 minute, 40 seconds.

Question: Is there anything else you would like to share as advice or suggestions to somebody who is trying to get an interview. Just getting an interview is a big thing.

Answer: I would say, as far as trying to get an interview, make sure, I keep on saying this, your presentation looks great. If you don't feel you are ready for an interview, just apply anyway. Because you never know what is going to happen. I have had it before where I have tried for a couple of places, didn't think much of it, and then three months later they call you up and like, hey, we're going to give you an art test or, hey, we're interested in talking with you. So you never know what is going to happen, just get your work out there even if you don't feel like it, or if you are shy, the more exposure the better. These people do keep your work on file.

Question: What did you wear to the interview?

Answer: That's an important question. For me, I'm not one of those people that will wear a suit and tie to this kind of thing, but, I will wear nice polished black shoes, designer jeans and a nice button up dress shirt with rolled up sleeves. So business casual I would say.

I would say some other additional miscellaneous advice I can offer is, a lot of people I've noticed get caught up in doing 3D in the art and craft and forget about everything else. But I do feel it is really important that as an artist, no matter the medium, if you want to get and be good at what you do, make sure you do more than just sit at the computer all day. You need to go outside, explore the world, because that's where you really absorb information and become a better artist. We're all in the industry to mimic reality or make something believable. I think it's important, to go out and do a variety of things besides just your artwork, because that's how you become a better person and a better artist.

Practical advice I can give is make sure you take care of yourself because sitting at the computer can cause problems if that is all that you do day-in and day-out. You have to do something for you.

Question: So what do you do for you?

Answer: For me specifically, I go to the gym quite often. Another hobby I'm getting into is actually breakdancing. A little random thing but, you know, I like doing things for me. Because if I don't work, nothing else I do will work either.

I think another big thing besides having a little variety in life, probably the most important element I would say to any form of success, is time management. You have to plan everything out, whether you need to write it down or just keep track of it in your head. You need a little time to just sit down and think about what you need to do, give yourself time to organize everything because if you don't it becomes a big mess.

Question: What kind of questions did they ask you? Do you remember some of the specifics? Was there a question that made you really pause and panic a little bit and think about an answer?

Answer: No. I basically was thinking on my feet pretty quickly with all of the questions they asked. When I had an interview with PIXAR, they said I needed more content, which kind of caught me by surprise, because I've had instructors here tell me I should take things out of my reel. So you never know what a studio is going to say because each of them has their own opinion regarding things. I had about a dozen different pieces and apparently that wasn't enough for PIXAR.

Cheryl: I always tell students, PIXAR is the cream of the crop. They can pick and choose anybody they want. They have that luxury of being extremely picky. But most of the studios do at this point because competition is so fierce.

Answer: I could say a little something about logos. When it comes to a logo, I do have a little freelancing experience in graphic design, and in my old school we were taught a little bit about that. I would say that if you are going to go with a logo, make sure it says something about you without saying anything. It needs to show a little bit about your personality or who you are as a person. For example, since we've mentioned Dreamworks, look at their logo. They have a little boy on a moon, and it looks like he's fishing for a dream. So I would it say it's good to have something that is implacable that says something about you because that makes you stick out a little bit, too. As far as your package is concerned, I think it's always important to have something there that makes you also stick out. For example, someone was telling me about one of their friends who when they went out for their interview they put their resume and cover letter in something that looked like a stick of dynamite. When the company got it, it would be like saying, I'm dynamite, I'm the one you want. So that's kind of an interesting thing. For me, what I'm thinking about doing for my next business card it's going to have all my information on the front, and on the back it's going to have instructions as to how to fold it up. After you fold it up it's going to be in the shape of a little cube or a box and all my information is going to be on the outside. It's almost like thinking outside the box. I think it's just a good thing to do something that's interesting. Something that makes you pop-out. Whether it's your logo, or how you present your portfolio. You don't always have to be traditional and follow the exact line. Break away from that.

Question: How do you feel about spending more time on your presentation materials and less time on your actual work?

Answer: I feel that if you do not spend enough time in all areas, it is a problem. For example, you have a really nice reel but you don't put enough time in the DVD or the resume. Some companies might scratch their head or question and say, "ok, they didn't really care about this as their portfolio." They might think that you slapped it together and didn't take the time and care into it. Obviously your reel is the most important content. I cannot stress enough you must have good stuff or otherwise they won't even hire you. I also feel if you are going to go to a company, everything about you needs to be tightly packaged, nice, and polished. That's just how I feel and that's what has worked for me in the past.

When targeting studios, the size of the studio is really important depending on what you want to do. The bigger studios, like Pixar, Dreamworks, Digital Domain, and ILM, want you to specialize. They want you to fit somewhere specifically in their pipeline. Whereas the medium to smaller size studios are much more generalized, because they don't have the budget or manpower to categorize everyone. Depending on what you are going for, if you like variety and you get bored doing the same thing all the time maybe you want to go for a smaller studio. If your dream is to work for PIXAR and work on Toy Story or something like that you need to specialize. Make sure your body of work is packaged in such a way for your future potential employer.

Question: How do you feel coming to a school like SCAD has helped you in this process?

Answer: I would say it helped me on several different fronts. First, I've been able to gain a lot of technical skills that my previous college just didn't offer. It's nice to go deeper. The software and resources here are also a plus. Everything from Renderman to Houdini, Maya, Mudbox—a huge variety of tools for us to use. They even have cameras in the cage. They have HDR chrome balls. It's great.

A huge thing that is overlooked elsewhere is networking. Sometimes you meet people here when they come in to interview. You never know who is going to come in here to the school. It's a great way to just come in and talk with them, maybe go out for some coffee, whatever. It's a great way to network around and get your name out there, and get to know people. Then there are your fellow classmates. Some of them are going to end up working at those studios before you, so, if you are buddy buddies with them then perhaps they can help you get your foot into the door.

Digital Domain, when they interviewed me, wanted to know who that I knew that worked for them. Then when I listed some names, said they were going to go back and talk to them. They want to make sure this guy (me) doesn't get mad when he's at the computer alone. How does he handle stress? It's good to have friends and be nice to people.

Figure A.2 The Desolo Aura

AN INTERVIEW WITH NINJANEER STUDIOS

Founded in 2010, Ninjaneer Studios™ is the collective brain-child of Joseph
Rosa, Heather Knott, and Christopher Brown. All three were students of mine
in the 2011 cohort at the University of Central Florida Character Animation
specialization (at the time it was called the Visual Language program).
I interviewed Heather and Chris, because they were insistent on Ninjaneer
Studios continuing the tradition of paying it forward. They felt that you
could learn from the mistakes that they have made. You can check out their
current work on the studio website at http://ninjaneerstudios.com/.

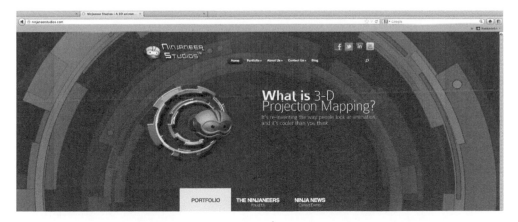

Figure A.3 Website of Ninjaneer Studios

Timeline:

Created LLC	September 2010
Began work	June 2011
Incubator program 6 week class begins	January 2012
After succeeding with their final pitch,	
Moved into office building at the end of	February 2012

Figure A.4 Founding Owners of Ninjaneer Studios, Joseph Rosa, Heather Knott, and Christopher Brown

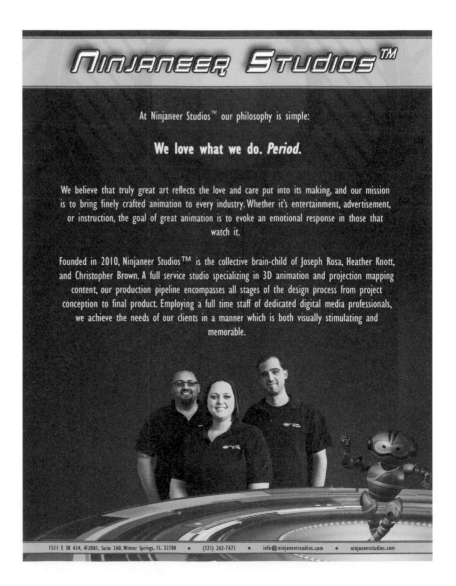

Question: What made you want to start your own business?

Heather: It actually initially started between Joe and I chatting about how, we didn't want to move to California, and we didn't want to spend the next 25–30 years of our life working for someone else. We had so many ideas. We had been talking about so many different shorts that we wanted to do and different ideas for different projects. Part of it was us not wanting to feel stifled. Also, the ability to create something on your own, to do it on your own, to stand on your own and say I made this from nothing. It kind of generated from there. From him and I talking, to him saying, "well are you in?" and we went from there.

Chris: It kind of happened very suddenly. I started rigging for them on Clockworks (an animated short they were working on) back when it was just a summer project. I started rigging and doing technical stuff for Clockworks.

The night Joe signed up for the LLC, he called me and asked me if I wanted to be on the LLC as a partner. I was kind of on the fence because I didn't want to leave him or Heather hanging. I wasn't sure I wanted to try to do the self-employment thing. The guy I worked for back in Tallahassee, a job I got when I was in high school as an intern and did some 3D work there, gave me one piece of advice. He said, "When you graduate, don't go into business for yourself."

Question: Why?

Chris: Because it is a real pain in the ass. It is what he did. He graduated and started his own studio and it is still there. It is a headache. And it is a headache. It is a fun headache.

Cheryl: I think no matter what you go into it is going to be a headache. It is more of, who's headache do you want to burden? Yours or someone else's?

Heather: To be honest there was a part of me that didn't count on Chris being there for the long haul. Not because he was not being committed, but I really thought with his talent he maybe sent out a few applications just to see and then be picked up. I'm really kind of honored that he decided to stick with us. I really am. Just so you know.

Chris: Well it's an overflowing pond of problems. And that's the reason I do this in the first place. I really like to problem solve. The business itself, working on a really small scale. Pipeline. Having to wear all the hats constantly. You don't really get to specialize. I can't remember the last time I took on a real rigging challenge.

Question: You've taken on different challenges outside of rigging?

Chris: There are a lot more things I have to deal with on the regular basis and a lot more problems that arise as a result of that, that I have to solve. It puts you in a real sink or swim kind of a position. Which is good for me personally. The way that I am. I do a lot better if I go ahead and attempt all of this stuff, then we have to figure out how to actually make it come together. I think the three of us work really well that way.

Question: Heather, when you and Joe decided to start this company what were the steps that you had to actually had to take to legalize yourself.

Heather: Research. A lot of it was just getting on the computer and looking and reading how other companies started. A lot of what we looked into was PIXAR's background. They are the gold standard of our industry. Looking at what's available here in Florida. Who's doing what and what kind of animation companies were already here. Joe said, eventually, "Screw it. I'm getting the LLC." and jumping in. Filing the LLC paperwork. Paying the fee with the court and state of Florida. It's online. Basically like getting or renewing your driver's license.

Question: Were there costs involved?

Heather: Yes it was a $175, which Joe paid out of his pocket for the initial fee. The LLC was the big thing just to legalize us. Then from there it was actually starting to work and getting our partnership agreement signed. Even though we're in an LLC and we're technically legally covered. This just goes more in depth. We found a template that we got through the legal service LegalShield.com that we use, their website, and then modified it. We then ran it through them to cross all the t's and dot all the i's.

LegalShield.com is an online legal service. You pay a certain amount every month. They give you up to x number of document reviews, x number of specific advice here and there. It covers what we need now and within our budget.

Chris: The UCF incubator program was amazing. It's the number one thing I would recommend to check with your local university to see if there is a program in place. Your five year success rate goes from 23% of businesses that succeed on their own, up to 85% for those who go through a program like that: Access to resources, advising, community partnership, and networking. The big players are plugged into this thing. The incubator programs' basic idea is to generate jobs. Small businesses account for 90% of new jobs; Businesses under 10 employees. It is in the best interest of the community to be plugged into this kind of program because it stimulates everyone all around. It is access to those resources and mentoring, they have a fantastic network of angel investors that they have brought together as well. They can help people look for funding. Flexible term leasing. The physical space itself is huge. It's a big killer of startups. Getting locked into a 3- to 5-year lease into not enough space or space you don't need. Then you just end up paying for it. That can be a real burden on startups. The incubator program offers a 12-month lease, but it is free and open. You can exit at any point as need be. You can also expand and contract on the space that you are using. Their buildings are set up in a pretty modular way so you can just take down a float wall and you start paying for the extra space. There are seven buildings as part of the UCF incubator program in the greater Orlando area.

Heather: The one thing about the incubator is that it is such a popular program because of its success rate. We had to go to Winter Springs instead of getting the downtown Orlando location. You have to be flexible with your location. It's such a great opportunity. Our office is 27 miles away. It actually ended up being a great setup because we are only four to five offices down from the Winter Springs Chamber of Commerce. They like to work closely with the companies there. They offer incentives for companies who come out of the incubator program and want to stay in the Winter Springs or Oveido area. There are a lot of connections you can make. Once you go beyond the incubator program you can end up getting tax incentives.

Chris: Florida is actually proving to be very hospitable. We qualify for tax-exempt status on anything we buy for the company. Digital Media is an industry earmarked for stimulus.

Question: After the LLC and Partnership agreement, then what?

Chris: We finished our degrees and went into the incubator program. We got the LLC one term before we graduated. It was in place and ready to go so that as soon as we graduated we could hit the ground running. From there we started looking for jobs. That was and still is the hard part. We looked on a lot of contractor sites, looking for work. What I tend to find with those, the margin is suitable if you are an independent contractor.

Question: Did you consider being independent contractors or freelancers? If so, why did you decide on opening a studio instead?

Heather: I know personally it was how well we rounded each other out. The fact that our three specialties fit so well that I knew that the work that the three of us did together as opposed to individually would be so much more improved and would be so much better. To me, I saw us more as an investment. I knew I could go out there with my graphic skills, and I could get a job that way. To actually be able to produce the caliber that I want to do, I knew I would need assets that I don't have.

Chris: I never really considered being a freelancer. Doing freelance work. I have considered it now, when money becomes tight. It never really occurred to me because I really enjoy working in a team. So the chance to actually create a team like that and a pipeline was far too appealing.

Question: Looking for jobs, what techniques, what did you start with, what were you trying to do? Were you contacting different companies?

Heather: Cold calling was and is a part of it. Hard part is you have no reputation initially, whatsoever, so you call these people and they have no reason to want to give you a chance. And that is the hard part is getting and generating the first couple of jobs. I know that our biggest asset has been the relationships that we've made. That has been our biggest asset creating buzz about our company and getting our jobs. Someone would tell us, "I heard that this company is looking for this and that company is looking for that," or we got an e-mail.

We did all the signups on all the websites, the research, the cold calling, and one avenue we tried commercials and doing commercial animation, graphics, just looking for work. Right now, commercial animation is what is keeping us going.

That first job was a contract that came from an e-mail that you sent us.

Cheryl: It's not just what you know but whom you know. Just being in the right place at the right time. It was during the summer, I don't check my e-mail everyday, and I happened to check my e-mail that day. I thought this might be something for Joe, Heather, and Chris.

Chris: Our doors would be closed right now. We would not have a company right now.

Cheryl: Utilizing the university resources.

Heather: Being friends with your professors, understanding that the barrier is not really there; that we are all human beings trying to work in this industry. We are all professionals trying to work in this industry. Being open with the people that you know and that you go to school with. Telling them, "Hey listen this is what I'm trying to do, do you know anyone? Maybe I can pull you in on the contract," that type of thing.

Cheryl: Starting out, one of the things I tell students all of the time, is if you are hired on by a startup company and they promise you x amount of dollars and they stop paying you, then you need to walk.

But if you are starting a company with your friends you need to expect that you are not going to be getting paid for quite some time.

Chris: We have had amazing luck with the people that have worked with us and continue to work with us.

Heather: Everybody that works with us, except for one, are former classmates.

Chris: The three of us (Joe, Heather, Chris) are the only considered employees. We have a core of 8 or 9 total.

We do get applications. We make a point to let everyone know that we are not hiring right now, but if you send us your demo reel and resume we will keep it on file.

Heather: We make it a point to stay in contact with everyone, cordially. No matter what.

Question: Ninjaneer studios, where did you come up with the name.

Heather: It was in an earlier class, and our instructor, Dan Novatnak was talking about everything that he has done, and how he was a Ninja and could do everything.

Question: Did you ask him if you could use it?

Heather: I think Joe did. It is now a registered trademark.

Question: Can you tell me about your studio color scheme?

Heather: We experimented with our brand and look. It has evolved over two years. It was mostly up to me. I looked at the name of our company and the tone of our company. We are professional, but we don't want to be stuffy. We wanted to be quirky. Yes, we are technical. My first thoughts were steel, blues and greys. Yellow was to add a little fun to offset that. It's a lot about the personality of the company. That's how the colors came in. Mostly it was a lot of me going, "hey what do you guys think?" and they would go, "uh, ok"

Funny story about the Ninjaneer character, it was based off of my chihuahua. I couldn't figure out the head of the character. One day my dog just walked up to me and I saw the shape. So my crazy dog is our Ninja, which I didn't tell the boys until after.

Question: Is there anything you've learned along the way that if you could look back and tell yourself two years ago when you were starting this what would you have told yourself.

Chris: You have no idea what you are getting into. Noooo idea.

Question: If you knew now …

Heather: I'd still do it. As much as I don't sleep and sometimes I worry about how I'm going to eat, seeing what we did the first Otronicon event, seeing our creation up there, seeing the way people reacted to it. That was worth it. (A four-day event, Otronicon is a celebration of interactive technology using video games to demonstrate the future of how we live, learn, work, and play. Presented by the Orlando Science Center.)

Chris: Being able to hear the wow. Otronicon. Originally we were referred by Dr. Sung, another professor, and that was, has been, continues to be, the single best piece of advertising we've ever done, was just doing that event. We did not have to pay an exhibit fee. They gave us great space perfect for what we needed to do. It was weird. All of a sudden we hadn't heard a lot about it. They showed us the space we would have and said, oh it's in about a month. That got cut even more because we were wrapping up another job. So we really had a couple weeks to get it together.

Really that was the single greatest thing. We had a woman who came in and was talking about advertising and how to advertise and market your company and get your name out there and everything. I'm of the opinion that we've had a long hard walk uphill because it is a reputation based selection process. Clients, the kind of clients we want, they deal with proven companies or they deal with the person who did the other thing that they saw that they really liked. Your work is what really sells you. Any work that you can get out there and seen and spread around is fantastic. I guess as far as advice would go, do things like writing tutorials or releasing work or side projects that you've done that can get seen anyway to get your stuff seen and remembered. That has done more for us than cold calling or any other form of advertising.

Heather: if an opportunity like this comes up, then you know your next month will be pure hell. You are not going to get any sleep; you are going to be sitting at the computer 16–18 hours a day just to get this done. Understand that it is worth it. Do it. It is paying your dues. Being single makes it easier. Joe has a family and has to work another job.

Cheryl: What you choose to do with your time doesn't affect anyone else but you.

Heather: If anyone else involved worked outside we wouldn't have a studio. The others who help us, about half of them have other employment, we are not stringing them along at all. They understand that we cannot pay them, but we do intend to hire them and pay them as soon as it is possible. We pay what we can here and there when we can.

We were informed incorrectly that we didn't have to file taxes because we didn't make anything. Come to find out we have to file as a business even if we don't make anything. Individually you don't have to. Thankfully, there is a rule out there that for your first year as a business, if you mess up like that and you don't file, because you start accruing fees. We accrued something like 6 or 7,000 worth of fees that they were looking to slap on us. But since there is that rule they can forgive it one time. Joe was told in a recorded conversation and it was noted in their logs that we didn't have to. We had proof that we were fed false information. They are lenient their first year. After that, you have to file regularly quarterly taxes.

Be prepared to wear a lot of hats. I never thought I would do graphics. I never thought I would teach myself illustrator, or build a website, or any of this.

Chris: You got to have a confidence in your ability to figure something out or to find a way to make something work, that may or may not be part of your skill set that you already have. You need to be able to identify what you need to accomplish. You have to be confident enough to find that solution; To teach yourself.

The number of times we've looked at each other and said, OK, then sat down and said, oh my what are we going to do?

You do that every single day.

The industry we're in, there are different ways to do things, there is always going to be newer different ways to use this kind of a skillset. As a company I think what is going to prove to be probably the greatest things we've ever done, was to have the flexibility to explore other avenues past just the regular animation that we're used to doing. Since we've been getting into this projection stuff, the amount of clients that have been coming to us, that have found us through our work for Otronicon, is 400%–500% more clients, even if they are just maybes, or I have a little idea, than we were EVER fielding when we were dealing just in animation. We started playing with projection mapping randomly because one person was like, "can you guys do this, I saw this thing once. It was kind of cool" We said, "yah, sure we can figure out how to do that, no problem!" As a result of taking the risks, as far as time and money that we've had to invest to develop the solutions that we've used and are continuing to invest to try and explore other ways to implement that kind of technology or technique in a variety of ways from trade shows to the arts; All the avenues that we can possibly conceive of. But having that flexibility and running from that; being willing to learn. A gentleman in Nashville, Tennessee, who is interested in projection mapping

Figure A.5 Ninjaneer Studios

work, contacted us. He contacted us because we are literally the closest company that he could find. That's almost a quarter of the United States away as far as geography goes. We have a chance, more or less, to corner an emerging market, at least locally. That is all because we are willing to explore a new avenue that just kind of dropped in front of us. When you are in business for yourself you have to be willing to be malleable in that situation.

INDEX

Note: Boldface page numbers refer to figures and tables.

T - #0974 - 101024 - C224 - 235/191/12 [14] - CB - 9781138428584 - Gloss Lamination